D0623103

PORTRAITS OF SUCCESS
IMPRESSIONS OF SILICON VALLEY PIONEERS

For Cille and Frank —
Thank you for your
friendship and support all
these many years.

Warmly,
Carolyn

October, 1986

PORTRAITS OF SUCCESS

IMPRESSIONS OF SILICON VALLEY PIONEERS

CAROLYN CADDES

RESEARCH BY BARBARA NEWTON

WITH A FOREWORD BY NOBEL LAUREATE JOHN BARDEEN

TIOGA PUBLISHING COMPANY, PALO ALTO, CALIFORNIA

To my dad, Sammie Dearmond, the first inventor
and entrepreneur I ever knew

And my mother, Corinne Magrill Dearmond, who
provided us all with loving and moral support while
tending the house, the office, and the shop

Library of Congress Cataloging in Publication Data

Caddes, Carolyn, 1935–
  Portraits of success.

  Bibliography: p.
  Includes index.
   1. Microelectronics industry—California—Santa Clara
County—History.   2. Semiconductor industry—California—
Santa Clara County—History.   3. Computer industry—
California—Santa Clara County—History.   4. Executives—
California—Santa Clara County—Biography.   5. Success
in business—California—Santa Clara County—Case
studies.   I. Title.
HD9696.A3U53173 1986   338.4'7621'0979473   86-40032
ISBN 0-935382-56-9

Tioga Publishing Company
P.O. Box 98
Palo Alto, California 94302

Distributed by William Kaufmann, Inc.
95 First Street
Los Altos, California 94022

Photographs copyright © 1986 by Carolyn Caddes

All rights to this book are reserved by Tioga Publishing
Company and may not be reproduced **in any form** without
prior written approval.

10 9 8 7 6 5 4 3 2 1

CONTENTS

PREFACE

In 1977 I began a series of photographs called "Palo Altans," portraits of people of various ages, races, and occupations in the town where I live, Palo Alto, California. One of the first people I photographed was Frederick Terman, the Stanford University professor I had often heard called "the father of Silicon Valley." That 1977 collection also included William Hewlett and David Packard because they and their company are such integral parts of the community. The idea for the four-year project that resulted in this book began developing then, as I recognized that my community was part of a historically significant arena: a place known internationally as Silicon Valley.

I originally intended that these photographs would be an exhibit depicting local electronics pioneers. I planned to donate the portraits to the archives of the newly conceived Technology Center of Silicon Valley. When I decided to turn the effort into a book, it seemed appropriate to add biographical sketches. "Faces alone don't tell you much," Andy Grove had commented during our photographing session. Although I did not completely agree with him because I often just like to see what people look like, it did seem clear that for a book such as this, faces alone wouldn't tell enough.

After making several portraits, I came home with what my family thought were interesting stories about the photographing sessions. They advised me to keep notes and make those observations into a part of the book. I felt that was too presumptuous, but I did keep notes on the sittings, and, when the publisher reinforced this idea, I put my notes into writing. These observations became a major part of the text.

Perhaps the most difficult task in making this book was the selection of the subjects. When I began—with the goal of accurately presenting the people who created Silicon Valley—I naively assumed that "out there somewhere" existed the definitive list of those creators and builders. After considerable effort searching for such a list, I had to conclude that there was no scientific way to choose the subjects. I read a lot and listened a lot. Then I began photographing the people who seemed to have high visibility or strong recommendations from their colleagues. The book does not pretend to be a *Who's Who.* The long list of people I had photographed was added to and honed down by the publisher's editorial committee. As a result, the subjects in this volume constitute a subjectively chosen group. I wish the lineup included more women and members of minorities, but historically it didn't happen that way.

When writing people to request portrait sittings, I asked to photograph them in comfortable settings at their offices or their homes. I preferred homes, but one man expressed what I think may be an honest Silicon Valley sentiment: "My office is my home."

Although I hold a different political and social philosophy from many people in the book, I tried to approach each person without bias in order to present each one fairly. I found our differences challenging and the paradoxes fascinating.

Most of the creators of Silicon Valley are still active—or at least they were in 1982, when I began this work. For the biographies we gathered information from books, articles, annual reports, conversations, phone calls, and a few interviews. Each person in the book approved his or her unedited biography except the late Dr. Terman, whose biographer checked his.

A few of the people have changed fields during their careers. These have been placed in the section of the book most consistent with their early successes in the Valley.

Portraits of Success is not an exhaustive history of the local electronics industry or of the geographical area it has made famous, nor is it an exposé. This book is a photographic and biographical account that tells more than is generally known about the innovators and the inventors, the entrepreneurs and the powerful support people who created the world's premier high-technology center.

THE PEOPLE BEHIND THE PORTRAITS

One day, while working on this book, I remembered an afternoon when I was a little girl in East Texas. My favorite movie star, Gabby Hayes, was coming to the old wooden building where we all went to the Saturday picture show. We paid our nine cents to watch the movie and to see The Man, "In Person!"

I sat there wondering what on earth he'd be like, this celebrity. Would he, like his image projected on the screen, be larger than life? What would he say and do when he arrived? Why was he coming here to Henderson, Texas, of all places? And did Gabby Hayes have a real life, like my family? I found it hard to imagine.

The questions people ask me most often about the subjects of this book are similar to mine about that movie star: What are they really like, these inventors and entrepreneurs, these movers and shakers? What are the traits they have in common? What motivates them? How did they respond to a stranger? How much money do they have and what do they do with it? How many of them are divorced? Are they happy?

My portrait sessions with these people ranged in length from seven to ninety minutes and did not provide me with the demographic, sociological, or financial data to answer those questions. But I will venture a few generalizations.

The portraits in this book record bright, healthy people: energetic, driven, intense, aggressive, disciplined, and self-assured leaders. Some are sensitive and thoughtful. Are they ruthless? Probably some are. Most are workaholics, but when asked, all tell you that their families come first. At this writing, a few are retired and one is deceased. They thrive on the creativity, the challenge and the competition, the camaraderie and the victories. The continual rush of adrenalin is addictive.

Luck was a major ingredient in several careers. Good timing helped others. But given what these individuals did with that luck and timing, I imagine that they would have excelled in any case.

I sensed the tremendous satisfaction they must derive from possessing what Henry Kissinger called "the world's greatest aphrodisiac: power." People's reactions to them as they walked through their lobbies was remarkably like the adulation given entertainment and sports celebrities. The coddling by secretaries, the reverential stares of employees, and the simple awe of passersby was astounding and almost contagious.

In our society money usually accompanies power, and many of these people have annual incomes that approach or exceed seven figures. Even the academicians are far from poor; they consult, they invest, and they travel. How do they spend their wealth? Their homes and offices cover the spectrum of styles and tastes from outright opulent to almost ordinary. But all are certainly comfortable. Their children are educated at the best schools and universities.

Recreations range from the exotic and expensive (aviation, helicopter skiing, art collecting) to the simple and cheap (fishing, gardening, running). Many said or implied that what they enjoy most about their work is the creativity, which I believe can be a stronger motivator than the pursuit of power or money.

In answer to the question, "Are they happy?" I can only give my impression that they are "happy" more of the time than they are "not happy." Because of position and wealth, they have far-greater-than-average control over their lives. They can build a world around themselves, and that appears to be satisfying.

Beyond these speculations, it's impossible to know just what motivates and sustains these people in their fiercely competitive work. Such questions are complex, largely psychological, and beyond the scope of this book.

Perhaps because the divorce rate in the San Francisco Bay Area is approximately 50 percent, many people are curious about divorce and remarriage among these Silicon Valley leaders. Because I didn't gather much personal information (that wasn't my plan), I can't accurately assess their divorce rate. My impression is that the older men are still married to the dedicated women who grew up at a time when the usual expectation was that they be first and foremost wives, mothers, and companions to their husbands. My information is that about one-third of the people in the book have been divorced, so this may be a group that is more traditional than the Bay Area norm.

Often, secretaries have provided continuity. Some have remained with the same boss for more than a decade—twenty-eight years in one case. As a secretary of eighteen years explained, "These men lead such frantic lives that they need something stable. It's often a secretary or a wife who provides that stability and gives to their lives a sense of order."

Most of the subjects in the book treated me like an artist. A few treated me like a servant. Because of my Southern roots, I expect people to rise and shake hands when they are introduced. Not always so! But what a pleasure when John Wilson and Sandy Kurtzig walked out of their offices, down the halls, and into their lobbies to greet me, then helped lug my cumbersome equipment back to their offices.

In many ways, the celebrities whose portraits and biographies appear in this book are larger than life in terms of both contributions made and rewards gained. When Gabby Hayes finally sauntered down the picture-show aisle those many years ago, we kids all tried to touch him. What we felt was flesh and blood, just like our own. But I thought then—and still believe now—that, unlike us, he got all the free popcorn he could eat. ■

CAROLYN CADDES
1986

FOREWORD

John Bardeen

Here is a story told in words and pictures about the people who have made Silicon Valley known worldwide for scientific entrepreneurship and technological innovation. A pattern for innovation was set by William Hewlett and David Packard, who built their first product in Packard's garage. Through the influence of Fred Terman, then professor of electrical engineering at Stanford University, high-technology companies such as Ampex, Hewlett-Packard, and Varian Associates were established in the Stanford area in the late 1930s. The big expansion of high-tech companies southward from Palo Alto into the Santa Clara Valley coincided with the explosive growth of the semiconductor and computer industries in the 1960s and 1970s.

The first semiconductor laboratory in the area was established by William Shockley in 1955. He chose Stanford as the ideal place in the country to locate an activity based on research and innovation. Earlier, Shockley had been at Bell Laboratories in New Jersey as cohead of the solid state department, formed in 1945 to exploit the understanding of solids from their atomic and electronic structure, an understanding made possible by quantum mechanics. These scientists hoped to fabricate new materials that could be used to make completely new components of communication systems. The invention of the transistor in 1947 by Shockley, Walter Brattain, and me was the first important product of this research program.

Shockley and I were in the first generation of students in the United States with training in the quantum theory of solids, and Brattain was an experimentalist with an extensive background in semiconductors. The crucial experiments were done in November and December of 1947. The device was named by John Pierce, an eminent electrical engineer who was then at Bell and is presently at Stanford's Computer Music Center. When asked by Brattain for suggestions, Pierce thought of the property of transfer resistance, because the first device operated by transferring current from a low-resistance input to a high-resistance output. He thought of "transresistor" and then abbreviated it to

"transistor." Brattain said, "That's it," and it has been ever since.

Like the vacuum tube it ultimately replaced, a transistor is an electrical valve; its entire action takes place within a tiny region in a semiconductor, usually silicon. In its simplest form there are three electrical contacts: a voltage applied to one is used to control the flow of current and power between the other two. The first devices were crude and expensive, so it was difficult to predict how widely they would be used. Many people contributed to the tremendous advances made over the years, advances that could not have been foreseen or even imagined. It was necessary to learn how to make ultrapure perfect crystals, far beyond the limits of ordinary chemical purity, and then to introduce small concentrations of foreign elements to control the electrical properties in regions far smaller than a human hair.

When I talked with my grandson, then six years old, about the invention, he asked a good question: "How did other people learn about the transistor?" Knowing Andrew, I knew that he meant understanding how it works. It was not an easy problem. Few people were knowledgeable about semiconductors, and most of those were in industry. Diffusion of knowledge about the science and technology required articles, books, and courses. Perhaps most important was the transfer of people to start new centers of activity—like Silicon Valley—at universities and in industry. With much of the resulting growth coming from one company spawning another, Silicon Valley is an outstanding example of this diffusion.

I talked with Shockley about his plans when he decided to leave Bell and set up his laboratory. One of his goals was to pick the very best people he could find, deciding that their increased creativity would far exceed whatever premium he might have to pay to get them. He searched the world to assemble the outstanding group that became the nucleus of Silicon Valley. Along with outstanding talent came independent minds, and in 1957 eight of the best, including Jean Hoerni, Gordon Moore, and Robert Noyce, left to form the Fairchild Semiconductor Corporation. Just as Fairchild is a descendant of Shockley Semiconductor Laboratories, a

large fraction of the companies in Silicon Valley, including Advanced Micro Devices, Intel, National Semiconductor, and Supertex, are descendants—or descendants of descendants—of Fairchild.

It was at Fairchild, in the late 1950s and early 1960s that scientists discovered how to mass-produce integrated circuits (ICs) in which many transistors with associated circuitry are built into a tiny chip of silicon. Following Moore's Law (after Gordon Moore), the number of transistors that can be placed on a chip has doubled nearly every year; it is now around one million in a "computer-on-a-chip." With the cost of a chip remaining about constant, the cost of electronic products has dropped dramatically, and there has been a corresponding increase in applications.

Along with semiconductors there has been a parallel development of computers, one of the main applications for silicon chips. Silicon Valley has become a home for computer companies and computer innovation. Hewlett-Packard is the parent of a number of computer companies; for example, Steve Wozniak, one of the founders of Apple Computer, is a former employee of Hewlett-Packard, as is Tandem founder Jim Treybig.

The explosive growth in these fields has created a dynamic atmosphere. It has resulted in a new, informal style of management that can keep abreast of rapid changes in technology, fluctuating demands, and intense competition for both ideas and markets.

Through photograph and story, Carolyn Caddes has produced a historic document with her intimate portraits of the entrepreneurs and innovators who created Silicon Valley and, in the process, changed the world. ■

Dr. John Bardeen is emeritus professor of electrical engineering and physics at the University of Illinois at Urbana Champaign. His research on the electron-conducting properties of semiconductors at Bell Labs led to the invention of the transistor, which earned him a share of the 1956 Nobel Prize for Physics. He is also responsible for the theory of superconductivity, for which he shared the Nobel Prize for Physics in 1972.

[signature]

THE CAPITAL OF THE FUTURE

In the mid-1970s the world discovered Silicon Valley and made it into an instant legend that substantiated the best self-image of America.

Home of the computer on a chip and the first commercially successful personal computer, the Valley leaped fully grown into public consciousness as the answer to America's problems of a shrinking industrial base and growing unemployment. It was the birthplace not only of technologies that were reshaping society but also of a type of capital formation that did not rely on banks but instead drew its money from risk-taking investors known as venture capitalists. Together, the technologists and venture capitalists had found a method of creating an endless stream of innovation, spawning hundreds of new companies with thousands of new employees. These technologists and business people seemed to be a new breed, finding new ways of doing nearly everything.

If Silicon Valley is something special in the history of technology and capitalism, it's not just because of a collaboration between engineers and venture capitalists. There's more, but it's a hidden history, known better by the people in technology than those outside it. This hidden history is the story of the men and women whose research has produced a plethora of interrelated inventions in radio, radar, electronic warfare, rocketry, space travel, microwave communications, television, solid-state physics, computer programming, satellite communications, and robotics. Their workplaces have ranged from the defense firms, the university laboratories and the think tanks that characterized the early days to the small startup companies and big industrial firms that typify the Valley today. Building on their achievements, venture capitalists turned the amorphous suburbs of Santa Clara County, thirty-five miles south of San Francisco, into an industrial center that has transformed society with its new products.

FROM LIGHTBULBS TO AMPLIFIERS

While much of the Santa Clara Valley was still covered with orchards and grazing cattle, technology was already beginning to shape its future and the future of much of California. In 1881 Stanford University's first president, David Starr Jordan, dreamed of bringing the gifts of science to the raw lands of the West. He lured outstanding science and engineering teachers to Stanford and predicted that from their innovations "must arise the New California of the coming century." Thirty-one years later, a Palo Alto laboratory belonging to Federal Telegraph Co., a company that included among its investors Jordan himself, was the site of an important event in the history of electronics. Some even argue that electronics was born there in 1912 when Dr. Lee DeForest hooked up a new type of vacuum tube, which he had invented six years earlier, to some telephone equipment and a loudspeaker.

Lightbulbs and diodes, kinds of vacuum tubes, were both already in use in 1906 when DeForest invented what has come to be called the triode. He modified the diode, used for switching flows of currents and converting alternating current to direct current, by inserting a third electrode. In his new invention, which he called an audion or triode, electrons given off by a heated wire cathode first pass through DeForest's extra element, the grid, and flow toward the positively charged plate. Because the flow of electrons varies according to an electrical signal applied to the grid, the current through the device becomes a faithful but amplified reproduction of that signal.

In Palo Alto, DeForest used his new device to amplify various sounds and had an assistant broadcast these sounds out a window while he listened for them down the street. It worked: a small electrical signal from a microphone had been amplified by the triode and used to drive a loudspeaker to produce greatly improved sounds. A year later, still working in Palo Alto, DeForest showed that his triode tube could be used, as an oscillator, to originate signals as well as amplify them.

The triode introduces a key concept upon which the entire edifice of Silicon Valley is constructed: amplification of weak signals. Later, solid-state devices made of semiconductors such as germanium and silicon would amplify signals in an immensely more efficient way, but once scientists knew how to make any kind of amplifier, electronics could begin in earnest. In the 1940s and early 1950s, it was vacuum tubes, not silicon chips, that dominated electronics and the electronics industry in Santa Clara County.

"When I got into this business [around 1946]," said Ed Ferrey, the recently retired president and chief executive officer of the American Electronics Association, "people would say, 'What makes it electronic rather than electrical?' And I would say that it has a vacuum tube instead of being wired together. That was the cornerstone of electronics, and the basic work on it was done right here in Palo Alto."

The tube alone was not enough to make the Valley take off on a course of rapid industrial growth. Despite an impressive record of invention in the San Francisco Bay Area (the loudspeaker was invented in Napa and the first "all-electronic" television broadcast took place in San Francisco) electronics companies remained few in number until the arrival of Frederick Terman at Stanford University. Terman, an electronics professor and author of important textbooks on the subject, encouraged two students, William Hewlett and David Packard, to form an electronics company. It was one of Terman's many good ideas, and the company became the nucleus of the Valley's large electronic instrumentation industry.

In 1938 Stanford Professor William Hansen and Sigurd and Russell Varian invented the klystron tube, a vacuum tube that amplifies microwave signals. The klystron tube became the heart of a postwar boom in radar and defense electronics in general, centered around Stanford. In 1951, encouraged by Terman, the university opened the Stanford Industrial Park on campus land and leased it out mainly to high-technology companies, among them Varian Associates.

THE AGE OF SILICON

Meanwhile, research continued on the solid materials that would someday replace vacuum tubes. The vacuum tube consumed too much power, produced too much heat, had a short lifetime, and was unreliable. Throughout the 1930s and 1940s scientists tried to exploit the potential of a class of materials known as semiconductors, experimenting with a variety of substances with little success. The ability of semiconductor crystals to create light, detect radio waves, and change alternating current to direct current was well known through research. Then in 1947 came an invention that would change the world: John Bardeen, Walter Brattain, and William Shockley developed the point-contact transistor. The first transistor consisted of three small wires inserted into a bit of germanium, treated with different materials at the point of contact of each wire. The three contacts are analogous to the components of DeForest's triode vacuum tube. The crucial trait of the transistor is that it amplifies current like a tube but takes up less space and power and is cheaper. Just as crucial to the computer industry is the transistor's ability to operate as a switch, turning currents off and on in millionths of a second.

The Bell team's early research employed two semiconductor materials, germanium and silicon. Silicon Valley owes its name to the fact that silicon proved to be more suitable for solid-state circuits. Semiconductors are relatively poor conductors of electricity because they lack the abundance of free electrons that carry current in good conductors. But impurities can be introduced into semiconductors to add extra electrons, which can then carry strong flows of negative current; vacancies or "holes" in the material carry comparable positive currents. The current can be controlled by the application of voltages from the outside. The result is amplification: a weak signal applied to a transistor comes out a stronger signal, and the process is faster and consumes less power than a vacuum tube.

Shockley moved to Palo Alto in 1955 and formed Shockley Semiconductor Laboratories. There, as in laboratories throughout the country, major improvements on the early transistor were being investigated, and a feeling that important breakthroughs were near had begun to spread throughout the industry. Stimulated by their perception of the opportunities at hand, as well as by clashes with Shockley, eight of Shockley's employees left to form their own company in 1957. Backed with venture funding arranged by Arthur Rock, the model for the venture capitalists to come, the eight founded Fairchild Semiconductor, the Mountain View division of the East Coast's Fairchild Camera and Instrument Corporation.

Further research led to the integrated circuit. In the IC, as it is known, thousands of transistors and other electronic components (diodes, resistors, and capacitors) are created on tiny squares of silicon ("chips") by treating regions of the silicon with various chemicals. These components are interconnected by metal patterns, also on the chip, to create electrical circuits. Separating the metal from the silicon is an insulating layer formed on the silicon through a technique called the planar process, essentially an efficient method of coating a wafer with silicon dioxide. The planar process was developed in 1958 at Fairchild by Jean Hoerni, one of those who had left Shockley's company to form Fairchild. Eventually, Fairchild's talented group split to found their own companies, several of which evolved into the semiconductor giants of the Valley. The big growth spurt was on.

DEMAND AND SUPPLY

The new companies responded to demand from the U.S. space program and the defense contractors that dominated the Valley in the 1950s and 1960s. In the early 1960s the real action in the Valley was centered in the spy satellites, missiles, radar, advanced microwave detection, and communications systems built by local defense companies and the space probes being developed at the NASA Ames Research Center in Mountain View. Defense contractors required increasingly small components for the exotic weapons that were made in secret in their closely guarded factories and laboratories. The nonmilitary computer industry eventually became the dominant consumer of solid-state components, but that development came later. In the beginning it was the defense industry's insatiable demand for new electronics technology that was the principal market force.

"The economic growth of the country has been heavily dependent on federal defense and space expenditures," the Bank of America reported in 1969 in "Focus on Santa Clara County." "About 60 percent of total manufacturing employment is in the aerospace-electronics industries; in 1950, the share was only 13 percent." Bank economists showed the local aerospace-electronics industry's markets in 1966 to be dominated by government spending, which accounted for about 70 percent of the industry's sales.

As integrated circuits' commercial opportunities became obvious, new companies that made them or that made something needed to make them were being formed every few weeks. All these companies were using silicon for their chips, and in 1972 Don Hoefler, a writer for the trade paper *Electronic News*, began using the term *Silicon Valley* to describe the area. At first it was a rather self-conscious term, requiring a certain hubris to repeat with any conviction. But the phenomenal growth in size and importance of the area has made the term recognizable nearly everywhere. Outside northern California, a relative handful of people have heard of Palo Alto, Mountain View, Sunnyvale, Cupertino, and San Jose, but the world knows where to find Silicon Valley.

Fed by the demand for miniaturized components, electronics manufacturing grew so quickly that many stages of its growth in the Valley took place within the span of a single career. For example, Jack Melchor arrived in the 1950s, lured by a job with the county's emerging defense industry. A physicist, Melchor began his career in research at a defense systems company. Next encouraged by the company's need for microwave technology, he and three others started a microwave firm. In 1961 the defense industry's demand for a broad range of solid-state components led Melchor to form and manage a semiconductor venture. Later he became a founding investor in Electro-Magnetics Systems Labs (ESL), one of the Valley's highly secret defense companies. As a venture capitalist in the late 1970s, he helped finance several of the many companies that emerged after the introduction of the microprocessor by Intel Corporation in 1971 and the commercial introduction of the personal computer by Apple Computer, Inc. in 1977.

Only a handful of electronics companies had been established in the Valley when Melchor arrived here in the early 1950s. The place exerted a powerful attraction with its orchards and Mediterranean climate, nearness to the Pacific Ocean and the Sierra Nevada, and proximity to San Francisco and two great universities (Stanford and the University of California at Berkeley), but there was only a hint of the development to come. "Sylvania [an electronic defense contractor in Mountain View] was a major input to the valley," Melchor recalled, "because it brought a lot of people out to California with advanced engineering degrees and degrees in science. There was nothing over there in those days except that building, and across the street was Ferry Seed. Lockheed wasn't there. None of those buildings were there. There were just a few orchards. Things were pretty isolated. You didn't have the infrastructure for small companies built up to the degree you have now. The big population influx was due to Lockheed and then to Philco Ford [both defense contractors]. The U.S. government, through big defense systems programs, really built the semiconductor industry, because they were crying for solid-state devices and high reliability."

As the electronics industry developed, its specialized nature meant that people working within it benefited from being concentrated in a small area, where everyone was in easy reach of everyone else. Innovators bought their supplies from other innovators. The processes by which computer chips were made were as new and as rapidly changing as the chips themselves. It was logical that such technologies would, with sufficient demand, foster a powerful city-centered economy like those that by turn dominated Europe in the late Middle Ages, the sort of economy whose brilliant trade and manufacturing sectors reached out and touched all nations. People were drawn to Silicon Valley from almost every country in the world; and in the value of its exports, the Valley outranked some small nations. Because of the forward-looking nature of its technology, the Valley became a sort of "capital of the future," a small, select society that introduced one significant technological change after another.

THE COMPUTER CHIP

Among these changes one of the most important is the microprocessor. In 1969 engineers at Intel were asked by Busicom, a Japanese firm, to build a dense array of chips so that Busicom could introduce a high-performance calculator. In the process, engineer Marcian "Ted" Hoff developed a way to get the central processing unit of a computer on a single chip. Other chips contained a read-only, or nonerasable, memory for the program and a random-access, or erasable, memory for the data. In 1971 Intel negotiated the right to sell the chip to other customers. Some members of Intel's board questioned the idea of selling the chip commercially, but board chairman Arthur Rock prevailed and the board endorsed the venture. The microprocessor now is the heart of Intel's business, but more importantly it is the ubiquitous "computer on a chip" that has become crucial to modern electronics.

As more companies began making microprocessors, the price of the chips dropped dramatically, creating fantastic opportunities for those who recognized them. A young computer enthusiast named Steve Wozniak in 1976 bought a microprocessor for twenty dollars and used it to build a home computer. He and his friend Steve Jobs formed a company called Apple, which was making a profit by the following year, and had attracted venture funding. Apple Computer Inc. was the archetypal Silicon Valley startup of its time: its founders were young and idealistic, and their faintly subversive goal was to put mainframe power in the hands of the common

person; their company made tons of money; and it maintained a blue-jeans and T-shirt corporate culture. Somewhere along the way it made a right turn and ended up on Madison Avenue, but by then the culture of the whole Valley was evolving in other directions.

PROGRAMMER KINGS

The purpose of computers is to process information. In order to do that processing, they must be given sets of instructions called programs. Wozniak had designed a version of the popular programming language BASIC even before he designed a computer to run it on. After a pioneer period dominated by hardware development—by better tubes and chips and swifter and smaller computers—the Valley seems to have entered a period characterized by software innovation, for example, "intelligent" computer programs, computer music, computer graphics, and even robotic ballets. Robots themselves, mimicking human movements, seem more their programmers' creation than the inventions of mechanical or electronic engineers.

Even in this new era of software, the Valley has laid down a solid foundation for future growth. At Xerox Palo Alto Research Center (PARC) a creative group of individuals developed the influential Xerox Alto, which pioneered ideas later borrowed for the Apple Macintosh computer. Stanford's Artificial Intelligence Laboratory was run for years by John McCarthy, coiner of the term *artificial intelligence* and the man who invented LISP (for LISt Processing), a broad-based language that has been a key to research and development in the field of artificial intelligence. Expert systems, which replicate the decision making of human consultants within narrow areas of expertise, were developed at Stanford Research Institute (now SRI International) and at Stanford University. Computer graphics, another field that was initiated by the Defense Department and NASA, now is a field big enough to support several Valley companies, one of whose animations appear regularly on network television. The Valley is also becoming a center for a type of logic-based programming that promises software able to repair and update itself and even to write computer programs.

Innovation will continue here because the Valley is not just a momentary aggregation of financiers and personal-computer manufacturers but a community of intellectuals working on a common set of problems.

There are few places they would rather be, despite the overcrowding, high prices, and traffic congestion. For those lucky enough to have been part of the technological revolutions and evolutions that have formed the substance of Silicon Valley from the 1950s on, there is a strong sense that the Valley is an enchanted place. It is a natural gathering place for anyone interested in computers, just as the salons of nineteenth-century Paris were the locus of culture and achievement for anyone interested in literature, music, or art in that period. "One reason I'm here and not anywhere else," said Jef Raskin, conceptualizer of the Macintosh computer, "is that everybody who's doing things that I understand and want to work on is here. . . . When things get on that kind of basis, they can move a lot faster."

COMPETITION

Competition from abroad has recently appeared to cloud the Valley's future. Worried semiconductor makers have been alarmed by several developments, among them the marketing and manufacturing strides of Japan, a recession in the personal computer industry, and a slowdown in worldwide industrial growth with a concomitant reduction in demand for the Valley's special know-how. Because the Valley got into manufacturing on a large scale through semiconductors and personal computers, these developments appear as a threat to survival rather than a temporary inconvenience. No longer is there any guarantee (if there ever was) that any manufacturing industry will become the private preserve of a regional economy, whether it is situated in the sun-drenched high-tech parks of California, the steel towns of Pennsylvania, or the technology centers of Japan.

Although the Valley has been identified with venture capital, microchips, and personal computers, its real product is research and development, and its most important resource is the imagination of the people who have been drawn to it from all over the world. Now that Silicon Valley has reached a critical mass for continuing innovation, there is no sure way to predict what the region will bring the world next. ■

Peter Carey is a special assignments reporter for the San Jose Mercury News *in San Jose, California, and recipient of the 1985 Pulitzer Prize and the George Polk Award for International Reporting.*

PORTRAITS OF SUCCESS

ELECTRONICS TECHNOLOGY

Sheldon Breiner
Marvin Chodorow
Paul M. Cook
Herbert Dwight
Edward L. Ginzton
Robert M. Halperin
William R. Hewlett
H. Richard Johnson
David Packard
William J. Perry
L. Eugene Root
Arthur L. Schawlow
Frederick Terman
Dean A. Watkins
John Young

SEMICONDUCTORS

"Fairchild Eight"
Wilf Corrigan
James F. Gibbons
Andrew S. Grove
Jean A. Hoerni
Ted Hoff
C. Lester Hogan
Eugene Kleiner
Gordon E. Moore
Robert N. Noyce
Jerry Sanders
William Shockley
Charles E. Sporck

COMPUTERS

Gene M. Amdahl
Nolan K. Bushnell
Doug Engelbart
Edward A. Feigenbaum
Kenneth E. Haughton
Steven Jobs
Reynold B. Johnson
Alan Kay
Donald Knuth
Sandra J. Kurtzig
Robert R. Maxfield
John McCarthy
Adam Osborne
M. Kenneth Oshman
Alan F. Shugart
James G. Treybig
Steve Wozniak

SUPPORT

Tommy Davis, Jr.
Reid W. Dennis
William H. Draper III
Ed Ferrey
John Freidenrich
William R. Hambrecht
Franklin "Pitch" Johnson
Tom A. Kelley
Regis McKenna
Burton McMurtry
Jack L. Melchor
Thomas Perkins
Sandy Robertson
Arthur Rock
Larry W. Sonsini
John A. Wilson
Jack Yelverton
Ed Zschau

Sheldon Breiner [signature]

The son of immigrant parents, Sheldon Breiner worked in the family bakery in St. Louis, decorating wedding and bar mitzvah cakes and delivering pastries. He chose to attend Stanford University for two reasons: it offered the best financial support, and it was the farthest away from the demands of the bakery.

After earning a B.S. in geophysics in 1959, Breiner began to pursue his childhood dream of becoming an explorer. As a student at Stanford, he conceived an application of the geophysical magnetometer, an instrument that measures minute variations in the earth's magnetic field. Varian Associates agreed to provide support for his research, and he joined the company. While there Breiner earned a Ph.D. in geophysics.

Varian gave him an assignment he describes as the "most fascinating job anyone could hope for: to take the world's most sensitive magnetometer and find uses for it." With the instrument he has recovered buried avalanche victims, sunken treasures, and missing nuclear submarines. Breiner helped discover two buried cities: Sybaris, an ancient Greek city in Italy, and San Lorenzo Tenochtitlan, a 3000-year-old Olmec site in the jungles of Mexico. He also developed the metal detectors passengers walk though in airports.

Deciding to start his own company, Breiner founded GeoMetrics, which specializes in survey equipment and services used in the search for valuable mineral deposits. When GeoMetrics was acquired by Edgerton, Germeshausen & Grier, Breiner founded Paramagnetic Logging, Inc. (which develops oil well probes); Fracture Technology, Inc. (which provides equipment and services for oil well production); and Syntelligence (an artificial intelligence company specializing in expert systems).

Breiner lives with his family in Portola Valley less than 100 yards from the San Andreas Fault. He operates a seismograph in his basement to record earthquakes from all over the world. In his leisure time he plays tennis on a court, called Double Fault, located on the fault itself.

SHELDON BREINER

Breiner greeted me in running clothes at his hillside home. He had just returned from his "fifteen-mile morning jaunt" in the nearby foothills. An extraordinarily friendly man, he had a contagiously cheerful spirit.

We wandered around the house, deck, and grassy slopes to find the right spot for his photograph. As we roamed, we talked about his conservation efforts, focused primarily on preserving these hills behind Stanford. And we lingered on a mutual interest in photography: cameras, films, lighting—all of which he discussed in depth. Breiner has a good eye and easily found the best light for the pictures. After we took several rolls of film and drank some orange juice, he sat down on the edge of his deck looking out at the 400-year-old oak trees dotting the hillsides. He was relaxed and right at home, especially with his untied shoes.

Marvin Chodorow

When Marvin Chodorow entered the University of Buffalo as a freshman in 1930 he planned to become a lawyer, but a physics course changed his career direction. He became a physics professor instead.

At Stanford University he has educated and inspired a whole generation of scientists, engineers, and physicists who helped build Silicon Valley. His work as an educator and researcher has been important in the emergence of Stanford as an international research leader in physics and electronics. Chodorow developed the first klystron tube used in microwave relay communication systems, was one of the first members of the technical staff of Varian Associates, and has won numerous awards and prizes for his work on the theory and design of microwave tubes. He is a Fellow of the American Physical Society and the Institute of Electrical and Electronics Engineers and a member of the National Academy of Sciences and the National Academy of Engineering.

After earning his Ph.D. at MIT, Chodorow worked at Sperry Labs and then joined William Hansen and Edward Ginzton at Stanford in their work on microwaves. He and Ginzton designed the first multimegawatt klystron amplifier, making possible the high-energy electron linear accelerators at Stanford that are used in basic physics research and in cancer treatment.

Chodorow has a reputation as a sports fanatic—so much so that at a ceremony commemorating his thirty-one years of service to the University, one of the principal speakers was Stanford's director of athletics.

The only child of a Russian cabinetmaker, Chodorow early developed an interest in writing. "I won first place in a contest for an essay titled, 'Why Is Majestic the Fastest-Selling Radio in Buffalo?'" Years later, he heard Fred Terman mention that Majestic Radio had discovered the public liked bass tones emphasized, so they designed their radios accordingly. In response, Chodorow recalls, "I told Terman about my prize essay which gave some other presumably erroneous explanation for Majestic's popularity, saying, 'Fred, that was over thirty years ago, and I've finally found out the real reason Majestic was the fastest-selling radio in Buffalo.'"

MARVIN CHODOROW

I had heard that the Chodorows are gregarious and are regarded as intellectuals in a campus community of scholars. Although they had another appointment that Sunday afternoon, they patiently helped me move furniture so I could get my tripod into the right position. Dr. Chodorow even turned off the ballgame he'd been watching on TV. When I explained my love of clutter in photographs, they relaxed more and stopped buzzing around to tidy up. Leah Chodorow said, "If you think this is messy, you should see his office!"

I wanted to make one portrait of both Chodorows. Getting into the mood of the informality of the photograph, Leah offered to look even more relaxed by changing shoes. I was delighted when she asked me, "Shall I put on my Birkenstocks, dear?" The resulting photograph effectively captured that moment.

The Chodorows were such good conversationalists that I didn't easily learn much about them. They directed questions at me. I did learn that Marvin Chodorow met Leah Turitz when he was at MIT. They were married in 1938. They have two daughters: one is a sociologist and the other an actress. The Chodorows have lived in the same house on the Stanford campus for nine years, but in a wonderfully warm way it looked like forever. Knowing that her husband pioneered the research that led to microwave ovens, I asked Leah Chodorow where theirs was. "I wouldn't have one in my house!" she exclaimed.

P

aul Maxwell Cook is a pioneer in radiation chemistry. As founder, chairman, and chief executive officer of Raychem Corporation, he led that company to the *Fortune* 500 list in 1981. Raychem was one of the corporations cited for outstanding performance in the book *In Search of Excellence.*

Cook was born in 1924 in Ridgewood, New Jersey, where his father was a mechanical engineer. He was accepted to MIT before he was seventeen, but World War II interrupted his education. After serving in the army's 10th Mountain Division in Italy, Cook resumed his studies and received a B.S. in chemical engineering from MIT in 1947.

Two years later he joined Stanford Research Institute (now SRI International) in Menlo Park, California. While there, Cook started the Sequoia Process Corporation, which made wire and cable for the electronics and aircraft industries. "I had a determination to succeed," he says. "Business came easily to me and I could do a little of everything. I was the inventor, designer, and salesman."

With profits from the sale of Sequoia, Cook founded Raychem in 1957. After an initial success, the company experienced a difficult period. However, Raychem grew every year and is a business that now employs over 9000 people.

Cook and Robert Halperin, Raychem's president and chief operating officer, have become a team frequently compared to William Hewlett and David Packard. Both Raychem and Hewlett-Packard are working models of decentralized structure.

Halperin says of Cook, "From the beginning we hit it off. Through these nearly thirty years, there has been a minimum of disagreement. We think differently and reach the same conclusions."

PAUL M. COOK

We had arranged to meet a few blocks from Cook's office at his private indoor tennis courts. What a disappointment to walk into the vast enclosed area where I'd visualized the portrait and discover that the courts were being repaired and repaved.

Cook bounced in, very friendly. I elected to go ahead with the tennis court picture in spite of the disrupted setting. It had been hard enough to set up one appointment with this busy man. After he changed from office to tennis clothes, I showed him some photographs I'd already made for the book. He looked pleased, saying, "These are all my buddies. I'll be in good company."

We had trouble deciding how he should hold his racket, so he tried every conceivable grip including several that elicited laughs from the nearby workmen. Then he remembered his headband and slipped it on, messing up his hair but not bothering to look in a mirror. I continued snapping the shutter. Five minutes later he was again dressed for work, the wild-haired tennis player transformed into the carefully-groomed executive.

Hbn Dwight Jr.

H

erbert McGilvray Dwight, Jr., attended Stanford, a family tradition since that institution first opened its doors. His great-grandfather, a stonemason, had helped construct many of Stanford's buildings, including the Inner Quad and Memorial Church.

Born in Palo Alto, Dwight grew up in Southern California, where his father was an engineer with Southern California Gas Company. When a high-school chemistry experiment involving moon rockets blew up in Dwight's face, he decided that chemistry would not be his college major. Dwight received a B.S. degree in electrical engineering, then served three years in the navy. In 1959 he returned to Stanford for an M.S.E.E. degree.

After working at Hewlett-Packard and Varian Associates, Dwight joined Robert Rempel and three other founders in 1960 to form a company. With several friends, the founders scraped together $150,000 to start Spectra-Physics. In 1961 they temporarily joined forces with Perkin-Elmer to develop the first commercial gas lasers, which appealed to research scientists and found growing market acceptance.

Spectra-Physics solidly established itself as a premier manufacturer of the most widely used lasers. These highly directional sources of pure-color light became more and more in demand in applications that include construction alignment, land leveling, range finding, spectroscopy, and surgery. Spectra-Physics prospered. The company now has sales of almost $200 million.

Cofounder Rempel resigned in 1967, turning the presidency over to his partner. Dwight has continued to broaden the company's product base, expand overseas markets, and make acquisitions. A colleague says of him, "He is a good president because he is never satisfied with the status quo."

HERBERT DWIGHT

Dwight's secretary showed me into his large conference room to set up my camera. A tall, handsome, athletic-looking man with clear blue eyes appeared before I could get my tripod open.

The conference room seemed too impersonal to me, so I asked if we might use his office for the portrait. We walked through a nearby door into a wonderfully light, plant-filled room. It was spacious enough that I was able to move my tripod around easily.

As I positioned the camera, I asked Dwight about his flying. That somehow led into a pleasant conversation about his family. With typical fatherly pride, he told me about his two sons: Mark graduated from Stanford in 1982 with a degree in mechanical engineering, and Bill graduated from Princeton in 1984 with a degree in computer science. I was fascinated that one son would break family tradition by attending an Ivy League school.

Dwight sat down in his desk chair, and I told him I wanted a casual, relaxed look. "Lean on your hand and nearly go to sleep, but not quite." He responded perfectly.

Edward L. Ginzton

Edward L. Ginzton, retired chairman and chief executive officer of Varian Associates, has contributed to the growth of Silicon Valley as scientist, educator, business executive, environmentalist, and humanitarian.

Born in 1915 in the Ukraine to an American father and a Russian mother, both physicians, Ginzton was the only one of six children to survive the years of turmoil following the Russian Revolution. At age ten Ginzton built a crystal detector radio. Puzzled that it did not work, he stored it in a closet. Six months later, music suddenly poured forth. The radio had been functional all along, but until then there had been no nearby radio station.

When the family arrived in the United States in 1929, Ginzton spoke little English but graduated from Polytechnic High in San Francisco at sixteen. After receiving B.S. and M.S. degrees in electrical engineering from the University of California at Berkeley, he earned a Ph.D. at Stanford under Frederick Terman.

At Stanford Ginzton worked with Russell and Sigurd Varian on the klystron tube and its applications. Just before World War II he moved to Sperry Gyroscope in New York for further work on the klystron, microwave measurements, and radar for the war effort.

In 1948 he helped found Varian Associates, a company which now makes a variety of electronic devices and microwave tubes. With Ginzton's encouragement, the company developed the linear accelerator for use in radiation therapy for cancer. He helped create a cooperative atmosphere at Varian in which the guiding principle was employee participation.

Stanford University honored Ginzton in 1954 when the lab housing the Microwave Laboratory was named the Edward L. Ginzton Laboratory. He is a Fellow of the International Institute of Electrical and Electronics Engineers and a member of the National Academy of Sciences, the National Academy of Engineering, and the American Academy of Arts and Sciences.

"Grow and become educated," is Ginzton's philosophy, "but do not equate professional training with education. Try to learn how to think. Attempt to do what you want to do. Making a living is not enough."

EDWARD L. GINZTON

When I began this project I included wives in the series because I wanted to show the teams that produced the pioneers. I first photographed Ginzton with his wife Artemas in the livingroom of their contemporary home in Los Altos Hills. If I had been making separate portraits then, I would have caught her poring over the maps she is making of local trails and bicycle pathways. I would have made his picture among the fuchsias in their Thomas Church garden.

The Ginztons showed me through their house, where the rooms represent distinct interests or hobbies. In the livingroom was a collection of Southwest American art. The walls and cabinets of a study were decorated with photographs he has made over the last fifty years. Ginzton's office revealed—among his papers and books—several cameras, some now considered antiques. Three Model A Fords in the garage awaited restoration. But Ginzton's recurring interest was photography. He proudly showed me his darkroom with its new print washer. Owner of an extensive collection of Ansel Adams prints, he recounted his longtime friendship with Adams. "We had known each other since the 1940s," he said, "and enjoyed working together on several physics-related problems."

When I returned to photograph Ginzton alone, he again delved into so many subjects with his quiet enthusiasm that I left exhausted but exhilarated. That I remember fondly.

R. M. Halperin

In the fall of 1953, with no job prospects, Robert M. Halperin came West. "I'd been to California twice," he says, "once when I was eleven and for one day when I was in the air force. I knew I wanted to live near San Francisco." He took a job in the trust department of the Bank of America. He also worked with the bank's Small Business Advisory Service, helping to nurture startup enterprises.

After one year with Dumont Company in San Rafael, Halperin joined Raychem, the material science company that makes irradiated electrical insulation products. He and founder Paul Cook have built an international company that has plants and development laboratories in a dozen countries. Doing business in over 100 currencies, Raychem serves its customers from a network of offices in forty-five countries. As president and chief operating officer of Raychem he travels more than a quarter of a million miles a year.

Bob Halperin was born in Chicago in 1928. His father was an electrical engineer and his mother a concert pianist. He graduated from Cornell University with a bachelor's degree in mechanical engineering in 1949 and later that year received a bachelor of philosophy degree from the University of Chicago.

His first job was with the Electro-Motive Division of General Motors as an engineer. He left a year later to earn an M.B.A. at Harvard Business School. Later he served as a lieutenant in the air force.

Halperin works seventy to eighty hours a week and has little time for hobbies of his own but says, "I'm supportive of my wife's interest in art." His other outside project is serving on the board of trustees at the University of Chicago. "I'm deeply concerned about education," Halperin says, "and I give to that school as much time and money as I can."

ROBERT M. HALPERIN

A small bridge across a stream of pebbles led to the Chinese-style entry deck. At the two-story-high front door, Ruth Halperin invited me inside to chat and wait for her husband. Even on Sunday, Bob Halperin had gone to the office and was running late.

When Halperin arrived he burst through the front door like a whirlwind. I asked his wife if this was typical. "Oh, yes. He's definitely a Type A. Always was and always will be." I had met Halperin at parties and knew he was usually just returning from one trip and about to go on another. He often left those parties early to catch a plane. But his witty and penetrating conversations didn't leave anyone dangling.

At home he was the same. "Tell me, Car-o-lyn," he said, pronouncing every syllable in a way pleasing to my Southern ears, "what is this book all about? Where did you get the idea? Who do you think your market will be, besides all the mothers?" Finally he said, "I think you're onto something good."

After I photographed Halperin in the entryway, in his study with its overloaded bookshelves, and in the livingroom where a large tree grew in a gigantic pot, the three of us relaxed. We talked about Halperin's life. I had heard he had been a whiz kid. As he told me that afternoon, he didn't graduate from high school but went straight into the University of Chicago in a special program. Later he came to San Francisco. On his second night in town he met his future wife, Ruth Levison, at the symphony. I enjoyed watching them reminisce about their first date. The good-natured teasing was as fast paced and earnest as everything else appeared to be in Halperin's hyperkinetic world.

Will D Hewlett

As a graduate student in 1939, William Hewlett designed a resistance-capacitance audio oscillator for producing a wide range of pure tones. Earlier, in the mid-1930s, he and his college friend David Packard had thought about starting a company, but it had been the height of the Depression and they did not have a product. Hewlett's new design and the beginning of the country's economic recovery came at the right time to allow them to realize their dream.

The partners provided the original funding for the company—$538. They opened their manufacturing plant in Packard's garage. (That garage, at 367 Addison Street in Palo Alto, has become part of the folklore of Silicon Valley.) Walt Disney's purchase of eight of the audio oscillators for the film "Fantasia" put the small company in business. Forty-seven years later, Hewlett-Packard is a world leader in personal and business computers as well as automatic test equipment and electronic instrumentation. One of the most admired corporations in the world, the company employs more than 80,000 people, and is valued at nearly $10 billion.

Hewlett was born in Ann Arbor, Michigan, the son of a professor of medicine at the University of Michigan. In 1916 the family moved to San Francisco, where his father became a professor at Stanford Medical School. Hewlett entered Stanford, where both he and Packard studied electrical engineering under Frederick Terman. After a year of graduate work at Stanford, Hewlett went to MIT, where he received a master's degree in 1936. He then returned to Stanford to do electromedical research. Convinced that the talent and creativity of the young entrepreneurs would make a perfect match, Terman arranged for Packard to return to Stanford, and the Hewlett-Packard Company was soon born.

A private man, Hewlett maintains a low profile, shunning publicity. He is an enthusiastic fisherman and an expert on wildflowers. As a boy he also collected stamps, sparking his later interest in European history. Now semiretired, Hewlett serves as vice-chairman of the Hewlett-Packard Board of Directors. He and his first wife Flora, who died in 1977, set up the Hewlett Foundation to help support their extensive philanthropic interests. In 1985 Hewlett received the National Medal of Science from President Reagan, adding a fitting capstone to an honor-filled career.

WILLIAM R. HEWLETT

When I walked into Hewlett's office in 1977, we shook hands, and I showed him my husband's old hand-held calculator, one of the first made by HP—and the result of a project that Hewlett had personally led. With a delighted expression he said, "I wonder if this is one of those with the flaw in it." (The first production run had a subtle programming error.)

He proceeded to play with the calculator, absorbed in that miniature world. I enjoyed watching the man who had led HP into the development and production of this device acting like a child with a new toy. As he worked I reflected about the symbol of my generation of engineers and how it has changed: the calculator in the hand has replaced the slide rule on the hip. After a few minutes he looked up, smiled broadly, and said, "It has the flaw."

I asked him to roll up his sleeves for the photograph because I had read that informality was part of the HP culture and style. He willingly and laughingly cooperated. Because I felt I shouldn't take much of his time, we took pictures only at his desk. The calculator served as a good prop, something I seldom use. The first photographs I made were serious. Then without realizing what I was saying I blurted out, "Maybe I could see a good fisherman's smile!" And there it was. The fisherman.

HR Johnson

W hen asked to describe himself, Dick Johnson suggests that he is "mostly just ordinary." Yet he is president and chief executive officer of Watkins-Johnson, a company with more than 3000 employees and annual sales exceeding $210 million. He has published twenty-one papers, holds eight patents, and is actively involved in major community organizations.

Johnson was born in Jersey City, New Jersey, in 1926. His father was a mechanical engineer who designed fossil-fuel power plants; his mother taught kindergarten.

In 1943 Johnson entered Cornell University, where he studied electrical engineering. He received his bachelor's degree with distinction and was commissioned as an ensign in the naval reserve.

After completing his naval service and a year of graduate study and teaching physics at Cornell, Johnson received a four-year, all-expense fellowship to MIT, where he earned his Ph.D. in 1951. While at MIT, Johnson married a nurse he met on a biking trip, his wife Mary Louise. His first job was with Hughes Aircraft in Los Angeles. There he met fellow employee Dean Watkins, who became a mentor and friend and who later became a member of the Stanford faculty. In 1955 Johnson was promoted to manager of the Microwave Tube Research Department at Hughes.

The paths of Watkins and Johnson crossed again in 1957 at a conference on the Stanford campus. Over lunch, Watkins introduced the idea of starting a company to develop and manufacture traveling-wave tubes. Johnson expressed interest but voiced concern that they would need $1 million of initial capital. Two months later, Johnson's phone rang. "I've got the million dollars," Watkins announced, and Watkins-Johnson Company was on its way. The company continues to manufacture traveling-wave tubes, but its product lines have expanded to include amplifiers, oscillators, mixers, radio and microwave receiving equipment, and spacecraft transmitters.

"I'm a man who plugs along and tries to make things happen," Johnson says, "a man who has always been a little lucky."

H. RICHARD JOHNSON

His office seemed austere to me, but the Herbert Hoover presidential campaign poster was strikingly unlike anything I had seen in a Silicon Valley office. Johnson, soft-spoken and unassuming, talked about that long-ago presidential election, then excitedly walked across the room to show me an oil painting of the Stanford foothills.

During the year following that first photographing session, Johnson was extraordinarily helpful. He sent me articles and called twice to give me more information about Silicon Valley. His perspective and power of recall amazed me. As a result of his help, I added another person to the book.

I wasn't sure I had the picture I wanted and requested another sitting, this time of Johnson dressed casually in his home. When he met me in his driveway, I was delighted: this reserved businessman had turned into a cowboy—boots, bola tie, hat, and all.

After I photographed him in his study, we walked out into the courtyard with his baby granddaughter, and near the pool I took some snapshots of the two of them for the family scrapbook. I was touched by the sight of this frolicking, unguarded grandfather holding the baby in the air, cooing as only parents and grandparents let themselves do—unconscious and uncaring of the presence of a near-stranger's camera.

David Packard

As a Stanford freshman in 1930, David Packard met a fellow engineering student, William Hewlett. Their friendship led to the founding of one of America's most successful companies. From its beginning in 1939, Hewlett-Packard has been a solid partnership, with both men sharing technical and organizational responsibilities.

The company was incubated in a garage behind the Packards' Palo Alto home. Packard's wife, Lucile, served as secretary and bookkeeper. Both men enjoyed all aspects of the business—design work, production, and management.

Some of Packard's corporate philosophy was learned during a brief stint with General Electric, but most of it evolved as Hewlett-Packard grew from a tiny company to a world leader. The company's trademarks are a strong feeling of responsibility to employees, expansion from within, clearly established objectives, and a rolled-up shirtsleeves style of management.

Packard was born in 1912 in Pueblo, Colorado, where his father was an attorney. The young Packard read books on electricity, built a radio while in grade school, and later became a ham radio operator.

From 1969 to 1972 he served as deputy secretary of defense under President Nixon. Asked later if he might run for public office as a result of that experience, he replied, "I've thought enough about it to be absolutely sure I'm never going to do it." In 1985 he undertook further government service by accepting the chairmanship of President Reagan's Blue Ribbon Commission on Defense Management.

Packard is involved in numerous community and philanthropic activities. Sharing their daughter's love of marine biology, the Packards funded one of the world's largest aquariums, located in Monterey, California. Packard participated in the design of both the building and the exhibits. Completed in 1984, the project is an overwhelming success and has fulfilled the family's expectations of being both entertaining and educational. Like the Hewlett-Packard Company, the aquarium promises to set the standard by which others are measured.

DAVID PACKARD

I was nervous. Not because he founded one of the world's greatest corporations. Not because he's one of the most well-known men in the country. But because he's tall: at six feet four, Packard towers some fourteen inches over me.

When I had first photographed him in 1977, I'd been so nervous that I put my camera on my tripod crooked and couldn't carry on much of a conversation even though the man was sitting down and I was standing up. He had mercifully tried to help me by talking about photography.

Next time, eight years later, David Packard was better known, but fortunately not taller. And I was ready: I brought my ladder and had memorized a list of topics to discuss while in his office.

Naturally, one topic to discuss was the new Monterey Bay Aquarium. When I asked him about the wave machine he had designed, he skipped over that topic and started talking about the fish, and that evolved into fishing. I was delighted, because my dad used to take me fishing in Texas and had promised to teach me fly fishing when I finished this book. All my rehearsed topics of conversation went unused. We talked about which side of the rock the fish would be on when the current was moving around it; how one can cast from underneath a bush; what kind of bag to put your fish into; whether Idaho trout are as good as California trout.

This photographing session was one of my most pleasant and least hurried.

William J. Perry

William Perry was born in 1927 in a small steel-mill town in Pennsylvania where his father owned a grocery store. His mother, a teacher, taught him to read before he started school.

Perry received a B.S. and an M.S. from Stanford and a Ph.D. from Penn State, all in mathematics. He came to Santa Clara Valley to join Sylvania in 1954. Ten years later he founded Electro-Magnetic Systems Labs, Inc. (ESL), where he served as president. In 1977 Perry was appointed under secretary of defense for research and engineering. He says that although his Washington job was by no means financially rewarding, "it provided a generous psychic income. The opportunity to shape national policies is something no businessman should pass up."

Currently, Perry is managing director of Hambrecht and Quist, a San Francisco investment banking firm specializing in high-technology companies. He is also a director of a number of companies and serves as a trustee of Rockefeller University, the MITRE Corporation, and the Carnegie Endowment for International Peace. In addition, Perry lectures on arms control and disarmament at Stanford's International Security Center.

Mozart and Jefferson are Perry's heroes. "They were truly original geniuses—giants of their time or of any time," Perry says. "And their work seems as fresh and relevant today as it was in the eighteenth century."

WILLIAM J. PERRY

At the end of a long road and a short driveway, an elegant but unpretentious wooden house nestles in the hillside. Bill Perry answered the doorbell of his Los Altos Hills home, introduced himself, and invited me into the livingroom, whereupon he apologized that he had to complete a phone call. While I waited I had time to look around and noticed a lightly rendered sketch of Louie Armstrong, signed "Bill Perry." I later learned that his son is the artist. Subsequently I bought a print and hung it near my computer, where I often gazed upon it as I wrote this text.

When he returned, Perry showed me around his home and introduced me to his wife Lee who had just returned from the market and was preparing lunch for eight guests. We talked about his early days at Sylvania and his leaving industry for government. I felt he was glad to be back in his own custom-built home and garden on the West Coast—commuting several days a week to San Francisco—and glad to be back in the electronics industry.

When we came to his study, I saw several children's photographs sitting on his rolltop desk. "I have three grandchildren and another one due any minute." Two decades ago I had heard of Bill Perry as a hard-driving businessman and a loving father. Now I felt that at least part of that pattern was repeating with this new set of children in his life.

As Perry helped me pack my gear into the car, we discussed his latest reading, *The Fifth Generation*, a book about artificial intelligence. He also spoke fondly of his garden and its recent design changes. Pointing to several corners of his one-acre lawn, he spoke about it with such enthusiasm that I wouldn't be surprised if he mows it all himself.

L. Eugene Root

E ugene Root brought the missile and space business to Silicon Valley. After the war, Root was one of the first four participants in the newly formed Rand think tank. His work on long-term defense planning took him to the Pentagon for two years. In 1953 he joined Lockheed Aircraft Corporation in Burbank, California, and established a development plan for a missiles and space program. In 1957 Root was sent to Sunnyvale to build a plant to house such a project, and by 1961 he was president of Lockheed Missiles and Space Company. Still the largest employer in Silicon Valley, Lockheed is a national leader in sub-launched missile and space technology.

Root was born in 1910 in Lewiston, Idaho, where his father owned a candy shop. "When I was old enough to reach into the candy bins," he says laughingly, "we had to quit the business." The family later moved to California, where Root attended the College of the Pacific in Stockton. The scholarships he received weren't enough, so he secured a personal loan from one of his paper-route customers.

While completing his graduate work at Cal Tech, Root became absorbed in aeronautics. Arthur Raymond, assistant chief engineer at Douglas Aircraft, visited the campus as a guest lecturer and was so impressed with Root that he offered him a job. Root wanted to complete his Ph.D. studies but decided that it was the right time to join Douglas. In 1934 he left Cal Tech with two master's degrees but one year short of his Ph.D.

World War II placed heavy demands on the Douglas design team, but they were also looking to the future, recognizing the need for aircraft capable of much higher speeds. A civilian naval assignment took Root to Germany in 1945 to document German wartime technical programs. The information he gathered proved of great value to military aircraft design.

Root is described as a methodical, contemplative man of high integrity who admits to his share of "just plain cussed stubbornness." In reflection, he says, "All in all, I have had a privileged career. I have seen the first small steps into new fields of endeavor that lie on the ocean floor at one extreme and the limitless reach of space on the other."

L. EUGENE ROOT

Gene Root was the Lockheed connection for the book, and only through patience and pushiness did I get his photograph. I waited until he had completely recovered from his latest heart surgery.

Root and his wife, Beryl, live in a quiet Menlo Park neighborhood in a home filled with mementoes from Douglas, Rand, Lockheed, the Pentagon, and their family. Books on history and space line the sitting room shelves. A closet-sized vault conceals his gun collection, including a hunting rifle his father gave him when he was a little boy.

I could visualize this strong, willful person convincing his superiors he was right in bringing an enormous aircraft company to the Bay Area and selling them on the idea of expanding the aerospace business. About his achievements, Root told me with obvious pride, "Lockheed brought the most to Silicon Valley first."

Arthur L. Schawlow

Arthur Schawlow has more than 2000 jazz records, a library of bird-identification books, and a file of humorous memorabilia he's written for scientists. He is also the coinventor of the laser and a Nobel laureate.

Born in Mount Vernon, New York, in 1921, Schawlow received a Ph.D. from the University of Toronto in 1949. His career has combined research, teaching, and writing. While a research physicist at Bell Laboratories, Schawlow spent a semester at Columbia University as a visiting associate professor and since 1961 has been professor of physics at Stanford.

Schawlow's research centers on optical and microwave spectroscopy, nuclear quadruple resonance, superconductivity, and lasers. With Charles Townes he coauthored *Microwave Spectroscopy,* considered the classic in the field, and coinvented the laser. Used widely in applications ranging from supermarket bar code readers to high-fidelity audio disk players, lasers are also used in Star Wars military experiments. In 1981 Schawlow received the Nobel Prize for his contributions to the development of laser spectroscopy. The Laser Institute of America established the Arthur L. Schawlow Medal for Laser Application in 1982. The first recipient was, of course, Arthur Schawlow.

In 1953 Schawlow married Aurelia Townes, the sister of his colleague. They have three grown children. Their firstborn son, Artie, is autistic, the focus of ongoing care and concern for the family. Part of Schawlow's reason for coming to Stanford was to search Northern California for facilities that treat autism.

Constantly seeking new knowledge outside the realm of physics, Schawlow occasionally takes courses at Foothill Community College in subjects ranging from birdwatching to foreign languages. After his first trip to China, he signed up for a Chinese language class but was forced to drop it in order to go to Stockholm for the Nobel ceremony. The college newspaper promptly featured an article on Schawlow entitled "Foothill Drop-Out Wins Nobel Prize."

A R T H U R   L .   S C H A W L O W

I found Schawlow to be a friendly, jolly man who works in an office overflowing with jazz records, papers, files, photographs, and toy laser guns. A recording of Bix Beiderbecke playing cornet reminded me I hadn't heard music in anyone else's office. I asked Schawlow when he became interested in jazz. "I started liking it when I began building radios in the 1930s. That's all you could get on the stations. I vividly remember the singular thrill in 1939 when I bought my first jazz record!"

The many things in his office—stacks and piles of "stuff"—fascinated me. I had no idea how he could find anything below the top layer. But as he rummaged around, he brought up joke stationery he had designed to help his colleagues who develop their ideas on the backs of envelopes. The envelopes have two backs and no front. They bear the logo of his mythical company, Doublethink, Inc. He looked under another heap of things and pulled out a sheet of authentic-looking stamps. The picture was familiar: Art Schawlow shooting his laser gun into a balloon inside a balloon. With obvious delight he said, "I wonder how far a letter would get if we used this stamp?"

When I was ready to photograph him, Schawlow offered to put on his coat. I told him this was an informal portrait and I wanted him to appear "as is," in his working or thinking environment. He seemed to appreciate my interest in showing the things we surround ourselves with as well as the styles in which we arrange them. I left the session in high spirits, feeling I had tapped into a reservoir of strength fed by a spring of good humor.

F.E. Terman

Frederick Terman earned the sobriquet "Father of Silicon Valley" by envisioning and encouraging its potential long before anyone else. He could also be called the father of Stanford Industrial Park, because it was Terman who promoted the creation of that base for research and commercial development, fostering the settlement of Hewlett-Packard, Varian, Watkins-Johnson, Lockheed Missiles and Space, and the many other technology companies that followed.

Terman did not attend school as a young child. His father was Lewis Terman, developer of the Stanford-Binet IQ Test, who advocated Rousseau's theories of natural education. When Fred Terman eventually entered grade school, he flew through in four years. He entered Stanford and received a degree in chemistry in 1920 and another in engineering in 1922. After earning a Ph.D. from MIT in 1924, Terman returned to Stanford to become an assistant professor in electrical engineering.

He soon came to bemoan the fact that his brightest students usually left the area for the East Coast. In the mid-1930s Terman encouraged two of his most promising students, William Hewlett and David Packard, to start a company in Palo Alto. In the years following that initial success, Terman would hold up Hewlett-Packard as an example to his students, advising them to consider starting their own businesses.

Partly at Terman's urging, Nobel laureate and transistor coinventor William Shockley moved his company from its small Mountain View lab to the Stanford Industrial Park. Shockley Semiconductor Laboratories provided a magnet for highly motivated and talented engineers, eight of whom later left to form Fairchild Semiconductor. In turn, Fairchild's offshoots laid the groundwork for other semiconductor device companies.

Always engrossed in his work, Terman found little time for outside amusements except some serious bridge playing. His former students recall him as tireless, with marvelous powers of concentration. Terman worked seven days a week and never took vacations. His explanation was straightforward: "Why bother when your work is so much fun?"

FREDERICK TERMAN

In 1977, when he was seventy-seven years old, I photographed Frederick Terman for a series called "Palo Altans." In 1982 I wrote him about this project. Enthusiastic, he consented to my photographing him at the Stanford building named in his honor, the Terman Engineering Building. Two nurses helped him out of his car and walked him to the front of the building. That 1982 photograph revealed his frailty and not his dignity, so I chose to use the earlier one.

What I remember about the first sitting is that Terman was formal, even ill at ease. To loosen him up I asked if he had a memento from the early days of Hewlett-Packard. "Oh, yes. I have the circuit diagram of the audio oscillator that Bill made in 1938. I'll show it to you." He popped up from his antique chair, rushed upstairs, and returned some minutes later with the diagram. He was less stiff, and he nearly smiled.

A day after I delivered a complimentary photograph to his Stanford home, I had a message on my answering machine. "This is Professor Terman. I like the pictures you made of me. I would like to get some more. Please let me know how much you charge." When I called him back, he asked, "If I order ten, will you give me a discount?" Eventually, I sold him a dozen archivally printed photographs at a 20 percent discount. We both won: he had enjoyed the game of negotiation, even though the stakes were small, and I had enjoyed his approval of my work, even though I lost money.

I'll always appreciate Terman's interest in this book. He died two months after the final sitting in 1982.

T he idea of my becoming an engineer," Dean Allen Watkins recalls, "probably came from a high-school teacher who recognized that I was good in all the right subjects." Born in Omaha in 1922, Watkins' hobbies as a teenager included building radios and working with electronic and mechanical gadgets. He attended Iowa State University, which he selected for its good reputation and reasonable fees.

During World War II, Watkins served in both military theaters. He was in Germany on VE-day and in Okinawa on VJ-day. When his service commitment ended he entered Cal Tech, where he earned his master's degree. After a year in Iowa with Collins Radio, he spent two years in Los Alamos designing test instruments. There he was able to work with the first transistors, which had just been invented at Bell Laboratories. In 1951 Watkins came to Stanford, where he received a Ph.D. in electrical engineering. During his graduate work he coinvented the low-noise traveling-wave tube, a device used in microwave communications equipment.

He then joined Hughes Research Laboratory, one of the premier facilities in microwave tube research and development. Watkins arrived at Hughes a few months before Richard Johnson and became widely known as a leader in the theory and design of microwave tubes. He and Johnson worked closely together until Frederick Terman recruited Watkins to teach at Stanford. There he developed his research ideas with the more than fifteen Ph.D. candidates who studied under him. By the time he left teaching, Watkins was a full professor of electrical engineering.

In 1957 Watkins and Johnson cofounded Watkins-Johnson Company, manufacturers of electronic devices and systems for defense and communications. When asked to define the partnership responsibilities, Watkins claimed that the two men initially brought equal techno-logical know-how to their organization and that over time they have both moved from technical to management areas.

Watkins' interest in education has led him to serve on local school boards, on the board of trustees of Stanford, and as a regent of the University of California.

Predicting Silicon Valley's future, Watkins says, "Production jobs will shift out of the area, and we will see not manufacturing but a new concentration of research and support positions."

DEAN A. WATKINS

Watkins' secretary of twenty-eight years, Louise Beer, let me case his office before he arrived. The out-standing feature of the austere room was a photograph of two horseback riders, Watkins and the then-governor of California, Ronald Reagan.

Watkins walked in. He was so tall that he had to bend over slightly to shake my hand. After the prelimi-nary civilities and a brief discussion about horses and the now-president Reagan, I asked Watkins to pose in front of that photograph.

Then I remembered that a display case in the lobby contained miniaturized models of Watkins-Johnson products, so I asked Watkins if he'd be willing to let me make his portrait there. I knew this meant he'd have to pose in front of people sitting in the lobby, but he agreed.

He was a good sport and entered the lobby after I set up the tripod. I had to stand on a ladder and extend my tripod to the fullest to bring the camera to his eye level. Even at that, he had to hunch down some.

WATKINS JOHNSON COMPANY

In recognition of Outstanding
Contributions to the success of

FIREFINDER

Presented 13 November 1980, commemorating
The Hughes Fullerton Firefinder Subcontractor Recognition Conference

J. H. RICHARDSON
President

HUGHES

N. YARU
Vice President and Assistant General

John Young

Although he modestly attributes his climb to the presidency of Hewlett-Packard more to good timing than to his own capabilities, John A. Young is nonetheless the person who succeeded the two superstars, Hewlett and Packard. When the founders stepped down, they chose an engineer/marketer from their own company to run the giant corporation. "When I joined HP after getting an M.B.A. from Stanford in 1958, I was one of the first new hires who didn't want to work as an engineer," Young says. "I was more interested in the business side of things, and at that time of rapid expansion my organizational interests came in handy."

In the business world, Young is considered a man with a strategic mind. Henry Riggs, Stanford's vice-president of development, a professor popular in both business and engineering subjects, and a member of several boards of directors, says, "If I chose the ideal board of directors, the first person I would pick is John Young. He brings quick insight and seems always to ask just the right questions." Since Young became HP's chief executive officer in 1978, company sales have more than tripled, to over $6 billion in 1984. Its work force has doubled in the same period, a sales per employee productivity ratio that reflects Young's careful attention to productivity as a means to achieve business success.

The son of an electrician, Young was born in 1932 and grew up in Klamath Falls, Oregon where he met his future wife, Rosemary. After receiving a degree in electrical engineering from Oregon State, he served in the air force.

Young likes to spend time with his family. They often fly—with Young as pilot—to their Oregon ranch, where they fish on what he describes as a "six-mile stretch of water that's incongruously called Five Mile Creek."

His friend Bill Swanson says, "John has a rare balance in his life, not only with his family and his work, but with his contributions to community and to government. He has been chairman of Junior Achievement, a member of Stanford's Board of Trustees, and chairman of the President's Commission on Industrial Competitiveness. He manages to make it appear effortless."

J O H N   Y O U N G

The drive from Young's office to his home behind the open expanses of Stanford's land is five minutes. Oak and eucalyptus trees indicate you've left the urban area for the country. The winding road passes ranch-style homes with stables and tall fences to keep the deer out. A tennis court spreads out on the hill below Young's new house. Full, colorful pots and flower beds planted by his wife greet visitors entering the stone walkway.

John Young looks like a 1940s movie idol, but he has none of the pretensions of a star. After he offered me coffee, we walked through his redwood and glass house, starting in his orderly study. I asked him where he had been working when I arrived. He took me into a warm, lived-in room where blueprints and papers were scattered on the breakfast table. "I've been working on HP business right here in my kitchen. It's the room where we spend the most time."

Light from the direction of nearby Windy Hill was streaming through the ceiling-to-floor windows. As I set up the camera and made several photographs, we talked about the recent visit of the Swedish king to Silicon Valley, Hewlett-Packard's three-year-old corporate headquarters, and Young's three grown children. I asked about his picture on the cover of *Business Week;* his daughter, Diana, who loves poetry; and his wife, who's involved in conservation organizations. John Young seemed more eager to talk about his family than about himself. From what I had learned about the man, that was no surprise.

Left to right: Gordon E. Moore, C. Sheldon Roberts, Eugene Kleiner, Robert N. Noyce, Victor H. Grinich, Julius Blank, Jean A. Hoerni, Jay T. Last

F A I R C H I L D   E I G H T ,   1 9 5 9

These eight men started it all. After leaving Shockley Semiconductor Laboratories in 1957, they banded together and founded Fairchild Semiconductor to pursue the commercialization of silicon transistors. On a base of silicon chips, they began building what was soon to be called Silicon Valley. From their company came two major steps for the electronics industry: the coinvention of the integrated circuit and the invention of the planar process. From Fairchild also came a new, informal management style, and later came spin-off companies that began filling the genealogy chart of Silicon Valley.

Getting these men together for a group photograph taught me how to be a highly skilled pest. I wore out Vic Grinich's phone-answering machine and wore down Bob Noyce's secretary.

Thank goodness they all cooperated. The effort began nearly a year before we made the photograph. I found it wasn't even easy to get the four locals together: Blank, Kleiner, Moore, and Noyce. Add Vic Grinich from Santa Cruz, Jean Hoerni from Idaho, Jay Last from Los Angeles, and Sheldon Roberts from Oregon and the difficult became impossible. After two sets of letters with fill-in-the-dates forms, I began to despair that all eight could ever be here at the same time. Then

one day Sheldon Roberts called with the news that he had a meeting at the San Francisco Conservatory of Music. After a few dozen phone calls within a few hours, we arranged a reunion on January 15, 1985, at the University Club in Palo Alto, for what we called the Fairchild Eight Silver Anniversary Portrait.

Eugene Kleiner had loaned me a portrait of the eight men taken in 1959. Wanting an "after" photograph to match that "before" pose, I tried to find the Fairchild logo that appeared so prominently in the original. The public relations department at Fairchild searched the basement and archives unsuccessfully for the metal symbol. Les Hogan tried to track it down. Bob Noyce's

Left to right: Gordon E. Moore, C. Sheldon Roberts, Robert N. Noyce, Eugene Kleiner, Victor H. Grinich, Julius Blank, Jean A. Hoerni, Jay T. Last

FAIRCHILD EIGHT, 1985

secretary thought Noyce might have saved it. "He's a real packrat," she said. She called him while he was on a skiing trip, but found he didn't have it. Finally, with a bottle of California wine, my husband persuaded a designer at his office to make us a foamcore replica.

Because I don't use a studio, don't like to use flash in portraits, and don't often make group pictures indoors, it took me several days of setting up and testing the lighting before I felt ready. Vic Grinich arrived ten minutes early and helped arrange the chairs and sofa pillows to resemble the setting of the 1959 photograph.

Another early arrival was Julius Blank, a man I had been eager to meet ever since he had filled out his date-available chart, signed it, and, disregarding my directions to fold on the dotted line, pleated the form into an elaborate paper airplane. A delightful example of the rebel streak that changed the electronics world, that airplane is an icon in my computer room.

For an additional picture, I had asked the men to bring props or symbols representing their recent work or hobbies. Jay Last, who flew in from Beverly Hills for the photograph, brought his just released book, *California Orange Box Labels*. I expected Hoerni to have his hiking boots in one hand, but he said they were too heavy to bring. Grinich had just returned from the Greek Isles and wore a Greek fishing hat. Sheldon

Roberts wore an aerobatic flight cap and jacket. Bob Noyce came in his Intel ski hat and carrying his ski poles, and Gordon Moore walked in with his fishing rod. In spite of graying hair, a few bald spots, and several paunches, these eight men looked like a group of overgrown boys.

But, entertaining as the photograph was, the portrait I chose for this book had to be the one showing the eight in the pose they had assumed for photographer Wayne Miller twenty-five years earlier, when they took the step that resulted in the name "Silicon Valley." ■

Wilf Corrigan (signature)

Wilfred Corrigan and his family survived the German bombings of Liverpool during World War II. By the time he was ten he was determined to escape the working class neighborhood in which he was raised and perhaps even to leave England. After receiving a chemical engineering degree from the Imperial College of Science in London, Corrigan decided his future lay in the United States, and he moved here in 1960.

His first job, with Transitron in Boston, launched his career in semiconductors. Motorola Semiconductor lured him to Phoenix a year later. When Les Hogan left Motorola to come to Fairchild in Mountain View, Corrigan was one of the so-called Hogan's Heroes who followed. He became president and chief executive officer before leaving Fairchild in 1979.

Wilf Corrigan's leadership style during the Fairchild years has been described as tough, demanding, impatient, ambitious, and cold blooded. In 1981 he founded his own company, LSI Logic. Whether he has mellowed with age or has tired of being perceived as a bad guy, Corrigan is now considered by colleagues to be polite, soft spoken, and people oriented. He commands fierce loyalty among LSI Logic employees.

Work dominates his life, but Corrigan does manage to jog and enjoy his Los Altos Hills home. To celebrate his company's third birthday he bought himself a new Rolls Royce—a fitting reminder of how far he has come from those early years in Liverpool.

WILF CORRIGAN

When I met Corrigan in his office, he looked different from photographs I had seen in *Electronic Business:* more slender and less formal. He was no longer what one journalist had called "cherubic looking." I learned that he had recently lost twenty pounds through a new exercise regime that was encouraged by his children, who had just given him a bike.

I relaxed when I heard his British accent. We tried a few photographs with reflections of Milpitas in the windows, then some with him standing in front of his chalkboard, and others with his feet propped on the desk. Soon we had the portrait. As I packed up, Corrigan and his PR man began to discuss the others in this book and the diversity of their backgrounds. Then they talked about Corrigan's early childhood. In order to work outside the home, his mother had to leave her young son, although he was only three. So she put him into a nearby school. Then, to help little Wilf pass for a five-year-old, she taught him to read.

Corrigan seemed to have been ahead of his peers all his life: as a little boy, as Fairchild Semiconductor's youngest president (at age thirty-six), and now as chief executive officer of a company successful despite the 1984–85 semiconductor slump.

Jim Gibbons

James Gibbons was born in a prison town. A Depression pay cut had forced his father to give up a teaching job in a one-room schoolhouse in Tennessee in favor of employment at the federal penitentiary in Leavenworth, Kansas, where Gibbons was born in 1931. From there the family was transferred to another penitentiary in Texarkana, where, Gibbons says, "I got a good East Texas education—English, Texas history, band music, and lots of sports."

Choosing electrical engineering over music and baseball (except for dance-band gigs to help with educational expenses), Gibbons earned a B.S. degree from Northwestern in 1953 and an M.S. from Stanford in 1954, followed by a Ph.D. from Stanford in 1956. He did postdoctoral research on a Fulbright scholarship at Cambridge University, then was hired to set up a solid-state electronics laboratory at Stanford. Gibbons worked half time at Shockley Semiconductor Laboratories and half time at Stanford.

The result of his affiliation with Shockley was an extremely fast start for Stanford in an effort that attracted a host of brilliant faculty and students, some of whom later started the Stanford Integrated Circuits Laboratory. In 1984 Gibbons was appointed dean of engineering, a job he has restructured to permit him to spend half his time on teaching and research. Those research interests have included semiconductor device analysis, process physics, and solar energy.

Gibbons has written or coauthored three textbooks, three research monographs, and over 200 papers. He is a member of the National Academy of Engineering and the National Academy of Sciences and is a foreign associate of the Royal Swedish Academy of Engineering Sciences. He has received the Institute of Electrical and Electronic Engineering field award for "pioneering contributions to ion implantation," a technology now used extensively in semiconductor device and integrated circuit manufacturing. He was also awarded a prestigious Texas Instruments Foundation award for an extensive record of "highly innovative research concepts."

When Gibbons called his parents to tell them about his appointment to the Reid Weaver Dennis Chair of Electrical Engineering at Stanford, his eighty-six-year-old father, who was still uneasy about a teaching career for his son, finally relaxed and said, "Well, I guess I won't have to worry about you anymore, will I?"

JAMES F. GIBBONS

On their twenty-fifth anniversary, his wife Lynn had given him a Richard Diebenkorn etching for his office. Fascinated with its geometry and rhythm, Gibbons hung it next to his chalkboard. "Go-lly!" he exclaimed in his soft Texas accent. "That painting reflects anything—*anything*—I write on the blackboard! Every formula I put up there can abstractly be seen in the Diebenkorn." Responding to that enthusiasm, I tried to photograph Gibbons between the painting and the chalkboard, but it didn't work. Knowing that music is a vital part of his life, I tried again at his home, with the trombone he's played since he was twelve years old.

The Gibbonses are so comfortable to be with that I could imagine sitting down with them for cornbread and a bowl of gumbo. Instead, we had a California chardonnay and talked about East Texas (Lynn is from Chicago but is patient with talk about the piney-woods heritage Jim and I share), photography, jazz, their musician-daughters and professor-son, Lynn's docent job at the Stanford Museum, and Jim's early days with Shockley and his respect for Shockley's analytical ability. Then we shifted to Gibbons' childhood. As he talked about his father, his eyes got slightly misty. It might have been the wine, but I don't think so.

A. S. Grove

Andrew Grove fled his native Hungary for the United States after the 1956 revolution and entered the City College of New York at age twenty. On the occasion of his graduation in 1960, the *New York Times* reported, "A Hungarian refugee who three years ago didn't know horizontal from vertical—in English—will be graduated from City College today at the head of the class of engineering students."

Grove received a Ph.D. in chemical engineering from the University of California at Berkeley in 1963. After five years at Fairchild Semiconductor he left to help form Intel Corporation, and his career began to skyrocket. He is now Intel's president and chief operating officer.

In addition to some forty technical papers and a textbook, he is the author of the bestseller *High Output Management* and is the personification of its credo. He also writes a weekly column on management techniques for the *San Jose Mercury News*.

As Andy Grove sees it, "If American industry could break down the walls between knowledge and power, we in the United States would begin to regain our lead in the highly competitive markets of the world." Grove admits he is a demanding manager. "If we were any less demanding of ourselves, we would fall behind. Complacency is probably the biggest enemy of anyone in this industry."

Grove's managerial style is controversial. Admirers describe him as brilliant, highly disciplined, persistent, and masterful in tracking information. Critics say he is hard-nosed, impatient, tough, and merciless with anyone who is less than honest. Grove sees himself as "blunt, but not abrasive."

Those characteristics, pro and con, prompted *Fortune* magazine to select him as one of the ten toughest bosses in America. To Intel's Tough Boss, that is a compliment.

ANDREW S. GROVE

Located in a corner with large windows overlooking Bayshore Freeway, Andy Grove's office is Intel low-key. It was one of the neatest yet homiest offices I visited, containing many memorabilia: a jumble of pens and pencils in a big mug, a picture of people dancing, gag awards for this and that, and crayoned pictures by small children.

I was more apprehensive with Andy Grove than with any other person in the series. Maybe it's because I had read he could be abrasive.

When we were introduced I asked him to inscribe a copy of his recently published book, which I planned to give my husband. He seemed pleased and I began to relax. A serious and intense man, he initiated conversation and listened so carefully to my answers that I felt he probably knew my pulse rate. We worked briskly. He asked if there would be any biographical information in the book, saying, "Faces don't tell very much." I had considered including written material, but his comment clinched the idea.

Andy Grove's interest in this book encouraged me. First he asked if he could use his portrait for his weekly newspaper column, then he offered to help me find a publisher, and he gave support through his secretary whenever I called. A tough boss? Quite possibly. A considerate person? Most definitely.

Jean A. Hoerni

As a child growing up in Geneva, Switzerland, where he was born in 1924, Jean Hoerni was fascinated by the American West. He spoke only French and German until he earned a scholarship to Cambridge, where he learned English. Hoerni received two Ph.D.'s in physics: one from the University of Geneva, the other from the Cambridge University. In the early 1950s, he received another scholarship to do postdoctoral work in Linus Pauling's department at the California Institute of Technology, and he experienced the American West firsthand.

Hoerni had planned to return to Switzerland after Cal Tech, but, he says, "I had become Americanized. In European universities you had to wait until someone died to get a good position. But, like Americans, I'm too impatient for that. So I stayed here."

After working as a research fellow in chemistry at Cal Tech from 1952 to 1956, Hoerni applied to Bell Laboratories. There he met William Shockley, who offered him a job at Shockley Semiconductor Laboratories in Palo Alto. "I made the right decision for the wrong reason," Hoerni says. "The right decision was to be in the semiconductor business, but the wrong reason was to join that particular company."

In 1957 Hoerni and seven other scientists left Shockley to found Fairchild Semiconductor Corporation. While there he invented the planar process, which dramatically decreased the cost of semiconductor devices. This advance fundamentally changed the way transistors were made and revolutionized the semiconductor industry.

Hoerni became vice-president of Teledyne in 1961, and in 1967 he founded Intersil, Inc. Later, as an independent electronics consultant, he worked with Union Carbide, Hughes Aircraft, Fujitsu, and Eurosil GmBH as well as companies in India and Singapore. In 1985 Hoerni received the Semiconductor Electronics Manufacturing Institute's highest award (the SEMI) for the development of the planar process.

Now residing in Idaho, Hoerni commutes monthly to his work as chairman of the board of Telmos in Sunnyvale.

Hoerni says he would like to be remembered for his contribution to the electronics revolution. "I can go into any semiconductor factory in the world and see something I developed being used. That's very satisfying."

JEAN A. HOERNI

I photographed Hoerni during one of his monthly visits to Telmos. He said he doesn't have an office there, so we borrowed someone else's.

From his accent I assumed he was French until he told me he'd grown up in Switzerland, two miles from the French border. Laughingly, he told me he'd been interviewed a lot recently. "With the press's discovery of Silicon Valley, I feel famous. All of us early Fairchild people are being discovered. I'm not sure how I should take it." This light-heartedness seemed to contrast with the reputation he has as a tough taskmaster in his various business activities.

Hoerni looked like the stereotypical scholar with his slight build and eyeglasses. I had trouble visualizing him in hiking boots and heavy clothing with a weighty backpack, trekking in the Himalayas, something he said he does nearly every year.

The next time I saw Hoerni was just a few days after such a trip in January 1985, when we gathered for the Fairchild Eight portrait. At the Kleiners' buffet dinner following the photographing session I was alone for a moment, when Hoerni joined me, asked about my work, and thanked me for getting the eight together to make their portrait. Still the European gentleman.

Marcian E. Hoff [signature]

When he was thirty-two years old, Marcian E. "Ted" Hoff put the computer on a chip by inventing the microprocessor. At that moment in 1969, the computer industry changed forever.

From his high-school years in Rochester, New York, when he won a trip to Washington, D.C., in the Westinghouse Science Talent Search, Hoff seemed destined to make his mark in the computer world. He received a B.S.E.E. degree from Rensselaer Polytechnic Institute in 1958.

Hoff spent his college summers working for the General Railway Signal Company and also working on his first two patents. He now holds fourteen patents and was named 1983 Inventor of the Year by the Peninsula Patent Law Association. His work in revolutionizing the computer industry led to his recognition by *The Economist* as one of the seven most influential inventors since World War II.

After receiving a master's and a Ph.D. from Stanford—picking up two patents in the process—Hoff turned to private industry at the invitation of the newly formed Intel Corporation. It was during his fourteen years there that he invented the microprocessor.

He then moved to Atari, Inc., where, as vice-president of research and development, he said he hoped to further the role computers could play in removing some of the drudgery from daily life. After Atari was sold in 1984, Hoff began working with a startup group, mostly ex-Atari principals, and doing some consulting. He admits, "Working under my own direction is a real test of my management skills."

At home Hoff has a complete electronics lab, including metalworking equipment. "I'm using my time to explore new ways to use computers, particularly household uses, and to improve human-computer communications."

TED HOFF

Why did I immediately like Ted Hoff? Perhaps because photographic posters by Ansel Adams and Brett Weston hung in the hall leading to his office. Perhaps because he told me he was a little tense today as he awaited a call from his daughter about whether she had been accepted to Johns Hopkins University.

I had expected the inventor of the microprocessor to be a highly academic scientist, but Hoff was down-to-earth and looked like the valedictorian–football captain from my East Texas hometown.

He stood up when I entered. He was friendly, talkative, relaxed. He seemed to like his life, even though he admitted it was hurried. His glasses gave me a bit of trouble with reflections while I was making the portrait. Considerate of that, he helped close drapes and block light, saying, "I apologize. The glasses cause problems for all photographers." We worked around the reflections and got the picture.

I later called Hoff's home and learned his daughter had indeed been accepted at Johns Hopkins but went instead to Pomona. During that conversation, Judy, Hoff's wife of eight years, said, "Ted is the scientist and I'm the music-arts person. But he likes everything. We're going to the San Francisco Symphony rehearsal tomorrow. We have a remarkably balanced life, I'd say."

C. Lester Hogan (signature)

In 1968 Lester Hogan stunned the business world by engineering a mass defection of the best and the brightest from Motorola Semiconductor in Phoenix to Fairchild in Mountain View. This group became widely known in the industry as Hogan's Heroes. When asked about bringing Motorola's senior staff with him to fill the void created by the departure of Robert Noyce, Charles Sporck, Andrew Grove, and others, he replied, "My mission was to get Fairchild back on track and return it to a profit position. That we did!"

Hogan grew up with four sisters in Great Falls, Montana, where he was born in 1920. Funded by scholarships and summer work, he attended Montana State University. During World War II he served as a naval officer aboard a sub tender in Pearl Harbor and Guam.

Armed with a Ph.D. in physics from Lehigh University, Hogan worked for Bell Laboratories, inventing the microwave gyrator, microwave isolator, and microwave circulator—devices used in radar. Following a five-year teaching stint at Harvard as Gordon McKay Professor of Applied Physics, he moved to an executive position at Motorola Semiconductor in Phoenix.

Hogan has been a professor, scientist, inventor, and businessman. Now in semiretirement, he is an investor and community leader. He serves on the boards of eight corporations and spends much of his time raising money for universities and civic organizations. Hogan says, "I feel I have an obligation to return something to this community."

C. LESTER HOGAN

A year before he retired, I made Hogan's portrait at his office in the handsome Mountain View Fairchild plant. Madeline Bare, his secretary, did indeed protect her boss. After she allowed me access to his office, I found myself studying a large wall covered with framed patents and awards. Stacked neatly on the coffee table were all the latest business, venture capital, and computer magazines along with several slick Silicon Valley annual reports.

I had first met Hogan at a Christmas party. When I told him of my then-incubating idea for this project, he suggested that I read *Revolution in Miniature*, an informative book about the electronics industry. It provided an opener for our conversation. Hogan deluged me with good stories of early Fairchild days. As he talked about people he considered pioneers in Silicon Valley, he whipped through an overstuffed leather address book that appeared to have been new back when the Valley was one large prune orchard. He scribbled names and phone numbers for me on a tablet.

"You just gotta talk to these people. They know a lot. They were here when this valley was virgin." His face became animated when he mentioned Jerry Sanders. "My wife and I are really fond of Jerry. He's like a son. In fact, Audrey refers to him as 'my baby.' She's very protective of him and won't let anyone say anything unkind about him."

Hogan was the first person who tried to explain to me the planar process (for making semiconductor devices). I left his office remembering only that the process had revolutionized the semiconductor industry and was invented by Jean Hoerni, a brilliant multilingual, multidegreed European emigré. Les Hogan gave me a keener insight into Silicon Valley's past and the entire field of electronics. I was fascinated by the affection people have for this man. In addition to Hogan's Heroes who accompanied him to California, his secretary moved from Phoenix to work for him in Mountain View—and has been with him twenty-two years, further evidence of the loyalty Les Hogan inspires.

Eugene Kleiner

After a successful career as engineer, manager, and semiconductor entrepreneur, Eugene Kleiner cofounded what has become one of the world's leading venture capital partnerships.

Kleiner's journey to Silicon Valley began with the German occupation of Vienna in 1938 when his father left the presidency of a shoe-manufacturing business to bring the family to the United States. With his schooling interrupted, the fifteen-year-old Kleiner became an apprentice tool-maker, learning the skill that helped him get a job immediately after arriving in the United States.

After his service in the U.S. Army, Kleiner passed his high-school equivalency exam and attended Brooklyn Polytechnic Institute, earning a B.S. in mechanical engineering in three years. He then acquired a master's degree in industrial engineering at New York University.

Kleiner had spent six years with Western Electric as a manufacturing engineer when William Shockley recruited him for Shockley Semiconductor Laboratories in 1956. The following year he and seven other Shockley employees left to form Fairchild Semiconductor, thus launching the first major successful semiconductor company and spawning the industry that put silicon in Silicon Valley. Kleiner stayed until 1962, when he decided to "do something completely on my own." This period produced his invention of Edex, a teaching machine designed to involve students in the learning process, and the founding of Edex Corporation, where Kleiner served as president and chief executive officer. In 1965 he sold his successful business to Raytheon.

Kleiner met Tom Perkins in 1972, and the two formed a partnership that eventually became Kleiner Perkins Caufield & Byers, presently capitalized at $230 million. They have financed more than ninety fast-growth high-tech companies.

"Venture capital has a special appeal to me," Kleiner states, "because of the variety and caliber of the people I meet." Kleiner and Perkins pushed to its logical conclusion an innovative, participatory investment approach. The partners bring their entrepreneurial and operations background as well as financial know-how to the process. Once they have invested, they participate in their ventures by serving as active directors.

Kleiner supports attempts to build "technological valleys" elsewhere in the world and is very positive about the future of Silicon Valley. "This valley is great—a place of beautiful climate, creative people, and excellent educational facilities."

EUGENE KLEINER

At first, Eugene Kleiner's low voice sounded stern, but after I'd been around him three minutes I felt he was a kind and helpful man.

Our first photographing session was held in his office, with Kleiner dressed in a very proper suit. It resulted in a photograph suitable for a very proper annual report. For my next attempt—at his newly remodeled hillside home overlooking Silicon Valley—he again appeared in a suit. As I begged for a more casual outfit, he told me, "I'm not a character." I suppose he was afraid I'd make him look absurd. Finally, he consented to remove his coat and tie, and I got the kind of portrait I'd wanted.

As I was packing up, his wife Rose joined us. We had a jolly conversation about her madrigal group and her reactions to Kleiner when they first met in 1947. "You should ask Gene about his singing! I fell in love with him because of his deep voice. I assumed anyone with a voice like that could sing beautifully. But he can't even carry a tune!" No use to the musical world, perhaps, but nonetheless a strong voice in the world of high technology.

In the early 1960s Gordon Moore made a prediction that proved accurate and durable enough to become known as Moore's Law. His original theory was that the complexity of integrated circuit chips would double annually. At that time, integrated circuit density involved only a few transistors per chip. The technology continued to improve, and by the late 1970s density was 16,384 per chip. Realizing that this pace could not be maintained indefinitely, Moore modified his law to predict a doubling every two years. Manufacturers began introducing one-million-bit chips in 1985. Moore's Law still holds.

Born in San Francisco in 1928 the son of a deputy sheriff, Moore received a B.S. and Ph.D. in chemistry and physics from California Institute of Technology. He was recruited into industry by William Shockley to work at Shockley Semiconductor. In 1957, along with Robert Noyce and six others (the so-called Fairchild Eight), Moore left Shockley to form Fairchild Semiconductor. He cofounded Intel Corporation (deriving its name from "integrated electronics") with Noyce in 1968 and became its president and chief executive officer in 1975. Four years later he was elected chairman of the board.

Intel's impressive growth and that of other American semiconductor device companies has been threatened in recent years by Japanese companies. Moore's special concern is that U.S. research projects lack sufficient funding. He is actively seeking government support in the form of a tax credit for corporations that fund basic research at universities.

Deep-sea and salmon fishing are Moore's passions, although he admits that most of the large fish displayed in his home were caught by his wife Betty. "At this point, I wish I had more time to plan and organize some fishing trips," Moore says wistfully. "The fish to go after are usually in remote areas, and a considerable effort goes into coordinating my schedule with the best time to fish."

GORDON E. MOORE

It's funny what you remember about a person and a photographing session a year later. The main thing I recall about Gordon Moore—besides his kindness to me—was his use of paperclips. In the course of positioning him for his portrait, I asked him what he usually does with his hands when he's not writing or on the phone. "I undo and reshape paperclips, like this." He reached over, got one out of his drawer, and looking me right in the eye straightened it and bent it back. The man probably rids himself of all his aggressions with the help of a $1.25 box of paperclips.

The conversation flowed so naturally that I felt I was not talking to a stranger. After a brief discussion about his deep-sea fishing trips with his wife we talked about the Fairchild Eight. He offered to help any way he could to get the group together for a twenty-fifth anniversary portrait.

Our brief photographing session was low key and comfortable. Moore's secretary of eighteen years, Jean Jones, skillfully put us at ease without intruding. A feeling of stability and calm permeated the atmosphere, small as it was, in that twelve-by-twelve-foot Intel cubicle. I do believe that Jean's office was larger than her boss's.

Robert N Noyce (signature)

More than any other individual, Robert Noyce put the silicon in Silicon Valley. He is coinventor of the integrated circuit, or microchip, and cofounder of both Fairchild Semiconductor and Intel corporations. These three contributions are at the heart of the microelectronics industry.

The son of a Congregational minister, Noyce was born near Denmark, Iowa, in 1927. He attended Grinnell College and graduated Phi Beta Kappa in 1949. After earning a doctorate in physical electronics at MIT in 1953, Noyce joined the Philco organization in Philadelphia. In 1956 he signed on as research assistant with the fledgling Shockley Semiconductor Laboratories. A year later he joined the Fairchild Eight who left Shockley to found Fairchild Semiconductor with funds from Fairchild Camera and Instrument. Noyce's coinvention of the integrated circuit in 1959 transformed Santa Clara Valley's orchards into the world center of high-tech industry and launched what some people call the second industrial revolution.

Under Noyce's leadership, Fairchild became the first successful semiconductor company in the Valley and the training ground for many of the entrepreneurs who later founded dozens of other companies.

His next move in 1968 was the cofounding of Intel corporation, a major leader in providing microprocessor and semiconductor memory technology for the information revolution. He is now Intel's vice-chairman.

Because of his work on a variety of semiconductor devices, Noyce received the National Medal of Science from President Carter in 1979, the federal government's highest honor accorded United States scientists and engineers. He is an articulate spokesman for the region's economic, cultural, educational, and political concerns. His leisure activities range from flying his own plane to madrigal singing and from skiing to scuba diving, according Noyce his reputation as a Renaissance man.

ROBERT N. NOYCE

Robert Noyce was one of the five key subjects for this book. I had photographed Terman, Shockley, Hewlett, and Packard. If I could get Noyce, I felt the documentary would be historically significant. Paul Hwoschinsky, a mutual friend, got me the appointment by pleading with this man who doesn't encourage publicity.

I had to be cleared by security when I arrived at Intel's sparsely decorated but comfortable lobby. Then Noyce's secretary came for me. We walked through a maze of cubicle-bordered aisles, and when we reached the last cubicle I realized it was Noyce's. As I stepped inside this small, ordinary working area, a smiling man stood up and came forward. Having read everything I could find about this local folk hero, I guess I'd expected a person bigger than life. All anxieties disappeared when I found myself face-to-face with a normal-sized human being who shook my hand like he meant it, as my dad would say.

Eyeing the ubiquitous little partitions that barely separated him from the others, I asked Noyce if he would just rest his arm on one of those short walls. He draped an arm up there and looked comfortable. He laughed when his reading glasses slid down his nose, and we got the photograph.

I asked him about his helicopter skiing, his flying, and his father the preacher. All three subjects were dear to his heart, but he seemed most animated when reminiscing about his father back in Iowa. Or was it my imagination—my wanting this man to appreciate his roots, love his family, and maintain the superhuman image I had conjured up?

P erhaps the real clue to Walter Jeremiah Sanders III goes back to Chicago's South Side, where he was born in 1936, the oldest of eleven children, and the son of a traffic-light repairman. His neighborhood was tough: Sanders was once stuffed into a garbage can by a street gang and left to die. He still bears the physical and psychological scars. Starting after-school work at age twelve, he became high-school valedictorian and earned a college scholarship. "That," Sanders claims, "was my ticket out of the ghetto."

Armed with an electrical engineering degree from the University of Illinois, Sanders headed for California in 1958 to the Douglas Aircraft Company. Later he moved to Motorola Semiconductor in Phoenix, then to Fairchild Semiconductor headquartered in Mountain View. There his talent for the Midas touch became apparent. Before he left Fairchild, he was worldwide director of marketing.

When new management came to Fairchild, Sanders was out. Perhaps he was too flamboyant for their more conservative style. With a year's severance pay from Fairchild, Sanders and some associates founded Advanced Micro Devices (AMD), the company he runs with a hand-picked management team. Sanders's corporate goal is to move AMD from number five to number one in the U.S. semiconductor industry by 1990.

"'Money is life's report card," Jerry Sanders claims, and money is the mainspring that powers his drive, translating into the material possessions that fascinate him. "I've worked all my life for the American Dream," Sanders says, "and now I'm living it."

JERRY SANDERS

I chose to photograph Sanders at neither his San Francisco nor his Malibu homes but at his Bel Air mansion. It was not Tinseltown-garish, but it was opulent. And it reeked of money, power, and sex.

Greeting me at the stately front door was a white-haired man, taller and younger than I expected—dressed in tight white slacks, a white T-shirt, and white running shoes: the Silver Fox of Silicon Valley. He introduced me to his staff and said they would show me around. I had been told that he wanted his picture made with two props, his white piano and a white marble sculpture of a female torso. Several of us lifted the sculpture into position on the piano top. I set up the camera while Sanders continued a meeting with his landscape architect.

While I waited, Sanders's administrative assistant showed me around the house. The heavy coffee-table books featured impressionistic paintings of women and fine-art photography of the nude female. The dazzling kitchen with all its lovely tile and stainless steel looked new and unused. The formal gardens resembled a movie set. But the bedroom was irresistible. To me,

that enormous four-poster immediately suggested Sanders's American Dream.

Eventually, he returned for his portrait at the piano. "Mr. Sanders, who plays your piano?" I asked. He said, "My decorator." After we made the pictures in the livingroom, I told him I had nearly used up my allotted time. He looked me right in the eyes and asked, "Carolyn, do you think you have the pictures you want?" Somehow I managed to say what I was thinking. "Well, Jerry, a dynamite photograph would be of you on your bed." He said, "OK, let's go!" So we rushed my lights and equipment up the winding staircase to the bedroom. On the way up he announced, "Good!" My AMD logo will show!" (That's the gold charm with his company's symbol Sanders is wearing around his neck.) He raced into his bathroom, quickly changed into a white terry cloth robe, and hopped onto the middle of the bed. When we finished photographing Sanders showed me pictures of his beautiful girlfriend. But revealing even more, he told me the names and ages of the special women whose photographs were on his bedside table: his three daughters.

W= Shockley

I n 1918 William Shockley's mother, a mineral surveyor, wrote of her eight-year-old son, "The only heritage I can leave to Billy is the feeling of power and joy of responsibility for setting the world right on something."

William Shockley was the only child of intellectual parents. His father, a mining engineer, died when Shockley was fifteen. Shockley earned his B.S. degree in physics at California Institute of Technology in 1932, followed by a Ph.D. from MIT in 1936.

As coinventor of the transistor in 1948, Shockley participated in one of the most important discoveries of the century. Then, by establishing Shockley Semiconductor Laboratories in Santa Clara Valley in 1955, he started the industry that later gave the area its nickname symbolizing high technology, Silicon Valley. He recruited his "Ph.D. production line," twelve select young scientists dedicated to researching the use of germanium and silicon for transistors. When he received the Nobel Prize for Physics in 1956 it was a thrilling event for his youthful employees, but not enough to quell pervasive unrest in his company. Disenchantment with pure research and with Shockley's management style led to the defection of the Fairchild Eight in 1957.

Shockley is passionate about his work: "It is my life." He frequently works at home throughout the night. In his life beyond work he has been a mountain climber, a competitive sailor, and a participatory citizen concerned with social and civic issues. For the past twenty years his controversial views on genetics have startled the world. He believes society may be evolving backward because of "excessive reproduction of the genetically disadvantaged." In spite of the disapproval of those who interpret his theories as racist, Shockley remains the undaunted optimist. He continues his efforts and research because he believes "the grave world problems that face us today will be solved, but not easily."

WILLIAM SHOCKLEY

One year after I first wrote Shockley to request a portrait sitting, I received a call on my answering machine: "This is Bill Shockley. If you want to take my picture, I'm available tomorrow at 2:30."

The next day at 2:25 I was in front of his one-story colonial-style home at Stanford. Emmy, Shockley's wife (and secretary) of twenty years, came to the door and cheerfully told me, "Dr. Shockley is doing his weekly gardening. He has thirty minutes he will give you." I was delighted to have that much time.

We walked down a hall to the well-kept garden. He met me wearing a straw hat and gardening clothes. Slightly stooped, he seemed shorter than I expected. He had a kind face and cleaner fingernails than most gardeners I know. He brought me to another section of the garden to see the three kinds of hybridized corn he was growing. Then he picked several ears for me to take home to my family. Before putting them into the sack, he ground up all the husks in his new Steinmex composting machine. Here was a man at play—a Nobel Prize winner, an inventor of the transistor, tinkering with his most recent toy.

After a few garden photographs, Shockley invited me into his computer room. He had built an ingenious stand for his computer paper to enter and exit its printer. "There's not another contraption like this!" he said. As he sat there surrounded by files, books, and printouts, I remembered a story I'd heard about his student days at MIT. They say he scrambled the wires on the elevator to deliver people to the wrong floors. I wish I'd asked him about that.

At the end of an hour, Shockley helped me load my equipment into my car trunk and with animated gestures told me jokes as we stood in the street. I was surprised I had genuinely enjoyed a person with whom I have a deep philosophical difference.

Sporck

My father was a taxi driver and gas station owner," says Charles E. Sporck. "Neither he nor my mom was able to go to college, but they were dedicated to the idea that my brother, sister, and I would go. We all three graduated from Cornell."

Born in 1927 in Saranac, New York, Sporck lettered in football, basketball, and track in high school, and, he says, "I always loved to read. I'm a ferocious reader." His boyhood heroes were the military giants of World War II—MacArthur, Eisenhower, and "of course, Patton."

Sporck joined General Electric's manufacturing training program in New York after receiving a B.S.M.E. in 1952. In 1959 an offer from Fairchild Semiconductor brought Sporck to California with his wife Jeanine, a librarian. He spent eight years as general manager of the semiconductor operation. "It was chaos," he recalls. Sporck left Fairchild to head the fledgling and struggling National Semiconductor Corporation.

Few companies can match National's record of success. "There's no excuse for failing to make money," Sporck once told an interviewer. Now president and chief executive officer, Sporck is a tough "manager's manager" who has led his company from a $7 million transistor maker to a $1.6 billion semiconductor industry leader in less than twenty years.

Charlie Sporck has been criticized by many for his blunt, tough management style. His no-nonsense business approach is exemplified by the fact that he commuted to work for several years in a pickup truck. Among current and former National executives, Sporck is either revered or reviled. Under his leadership, National has become known as one of the Valley's most hard-driving companies, described in *Electronics Business* as both a "go-for-the-throat company" and a "jelly bean juggernaut."

CHARLES E. SPORCK

Often what you get is what you don't expect, I learned over and over during the preparation of this book.

I thought I'd meet a harsh, perhaps even surly man, when I walked into Sporck's open and comfortable office. Instead, a large man with a great smile rose and shook my hand. He did, however, look imperial behind his enormous desk with its view of all the other unenclosed offices on the floor. Several tall plants softened the walls, reminding me that Sporck likes gardening. I visualized this military-looking man walking around with his watering pail, soaking the office plants and whistling, "When those caissons go rollin' along."

Sporck's spirits seemed high in spite of the day's headlines announcing that the government was examining the quality of some of the chips made by National for the Defense Department. Crisis did not seem to daunt him.

As we looked around for other locations for portraits, Sporck picked up a nearby mirrorlike object. "This is the biggest goddamned wafer I've ever seen!" Who could resist that for a photograph? But the finished prints made him look like he was primping in a mirror, not appropriate for the Charlie Sporck I met that day.

Gene M. Amdahl

While at International Business Machines Corporation (IBM), Gene Amdahl made computer history by designing the legendary System/360 mainframe. He later led Amdahl Corporation to success by starting the plug-compatible mainframe industry, manufacturing equipment that directly substitutes for IBM computers. He is now chairman of the board, president and chief executive officer of Trilogy Systems Corporation—the world's largest startup company, having raised $230 million before developing its first product.

Amdahl grew up on a typical South Dakota farm that did not have indoor plumbing until he was in high school. As a teenager he designed a helicopter, an early indication of his remarkable inventiveness and initiative. After serving in the navy during World War II, Amdahl studied at South Dakota State University on the GI Bill, then earned his Ph.D. in theoretical physics from the University of Wisconsin. His 1952 Ph.D. dissertation presented the design for a computer eventually named the Wisconsin Integrally Synchronized Computer (WISC), which was built by students over a period of four years.

After fourteen years with IBM, Amdahl founded his own company, Amdahl Corporation, which he led from 1970 to 1979. In its fourth year of operation, the company shipped $96 million worth of computers. When substantial amounts of additional capital were needed, Amdahl lost control of the company to Japanese investors.

Gene Amdahl then started Trilogy, which takes its name in part from the fact that it takes three faults or chip obstructions to cause a computer to stop working correctly. Trilogy was launched with dreams of building a superfast mainframe computer based on revolutionary superchips, large semiconductor devices that would perform unprecedented computational feats. Technical obstacles proved difficult to overcome, however, and Trilogy has been forced to shift focus from superchip and mainframe projects to integrated circuit development and packaging. Still cash rich, Trilogy has recently acquired rapidly growing Elxsi, a manufacturer of so-called supermini computers that are primarily targeted for use by engineers. One observer thinks Amdahl's "biggest problem may simply be that he is way ahead of his time."

GENE M. AMDAHL

I arrived at the futuristic Trilogy building in Cupertino and was taken into Amdahl's office while he was in a meeting. The exquisite antique furniture in his office made a marvelous contrast to the architecture.

When Amdahl entered he seemed shy, perhaps even a bit nervous. I asked him about his home state, South Dakota, and how a farm boy became an art collector. That broke the ice. He seemed proud of his farm upbringing. "But, we never discussed art of any kind. I hardly knew about the existence of museums."

This kind, quiet Midwesterner displayed none of the go-get-'em, eat-'em-up-alive competitive spirit I saw or sensed in many other Silicon Valley people. His personality had a low-key dignity about it.

After taking a few photographs, I asked him about his early work on computers. He smiled and offered to show me the one he designed at the University of Wisconsin, so off we went up to the third story to see this enormous contraption. He was so relaxed by then that I asked if I could photograph him there. My lights were in the car, but he agreed to wait while I went downstairs to get them. He got himself a cup of coffee. When I returned I found him talking to a Levi's-clad employee, both standing near the WISC. This computer—one of the first ever built—seemed to be his proudest possession, the symbol of his first academic breakthrough. I knew this was the setting for his portrait.

[signature: N. Bushnell]

Nolan Bushnell is a consummate gamesman who wins, loses, and bounces back. "I like getting companies started, not running them," he says. His ventures include Atari, Pizza Time Theatre, and Catalyst Technologies. The latter is an "incubator facility" with a dozen startup companies in such diverse fields as robotics, advanced color television, toys, games, and electronic car navigation.

One of Bushnell's recent involvements is Axlon, Inc., a developer and manufacturer of microprocessor-based toys. The products will be educational in the sense that Bushnell believes there is as much to be learned from playing as there is from sitting at a computer keyboard.

The P. T. Barnum of Silicon Valley made his debut in 1972 when he and Al Alcorn devised the table tennis-like game Pong, launching the national videogame craze. Atari, the resulting company, became the pioneering giant in the field, with sales of nearly $2 billion by 1982.

Born in 1943, the son of a cement contractor, Bushnell grew up in Clearfield, Utah. His interest in electronics began in the third grade when his teacher put him in charge of the class science project. By the age of ten he was a licensed ham radio operator. He attended Utah State and the University of Utah, where he received an electrical engineering degree.

Many of his peers view Bushnell as one of the most creative people they have ever met. One former associate says, "He is a spark plug—the source of the energy." A gambler and risk taker, Bushnell says, "Business is the greatest game of all. Lots of complexity and a minimum of rules. And you can keep score with money."

NOLAN K. BUSHNELL

Bushnell's office was the most unusual and sumptuous I visited. Everything was a deep, rich green, and the desk chairs, sofa, carpets, and even the walls and light switches were covered with a velourlike fabric. A large window admitted light on one side of the room, but the office was basically cave-dark.

After I had waited half an hour and absorbed the sensuousness of the place, a friendly bear of a man with dark curly hair and a matching beard arrived. He had a deep, pleasant laugh. I had spotted a trayful of pipes on his desk, so I asked if he would mind holding one for the portrait. He replied, "Well, I'd rather not.

My mother may see it, and she's a Mormon. It might bother her."

I had the camera set up to photograph him on his luxurious sofa, with a small robot on the coffee table in front of him. He sat there and put on the smile that I've seen in so many of his photographs. I wanted a serious portrait of this man as a contrast to the happy gamesman, but the open body language in this picture made up for the smile. I spent only seven minutes with Nolan Bushnell. I could have taken a little more time, but someone was waiting for him, and I thought I had the right photograph.

Doug Engelbart

During World War II, Douglas Engelbart was deeply impressed with an article he read in a Philippine Red Cross library—Vannevar Bush's "Memex." The article proved relevant to his career in computer science, because it suggested that ordinary citizens, as well as scientists, would eventually have to deal with processing large amounts of information.

Born in 1925, Engelbart grew up near Portland, Oregon. Learning to read opened new worlds for him. He considered grammar a marvelous invention, an attitude that probably led to his later interest in linguistic systems.

Engelbart earned a B.S. in electrical engineering from Oregon State in 1948, then worked at Ames Laboratory in Mountain View for what is now NASA. Rethinking his life goals, he committed himself to the possibilities of interactive computer systems that would bring immense improvement to human capabilities. He left Ames and moved to Berkeley, where he earned a Ph.D. in electrical engineering and computer science at the University of California.

In 1957 Engelbart joined Stanford Research Institute, now SRI International. In two years he was granted more than twenty patents in gaseous-discharge and magnetic-logic digital devices. In 1962 he published "Augmenting Human Intellect: A Conceptual Framework." The computer science community was not yet ready for the far-reaching implications of the report: that interacting with computers markedly increases the human ability to approach and solve complex problems. For the most part computer scientists paid little attention. Luckily, a series of people in the air force, Advance Research Projects Agency (ARPA), and NASA were instrumental in finding funds for the growth of SRI's Augmentation Research Center.

Engelbart's augmentation system was featured at an on-line, video-projected presentation at the 1968 Fall Joint Computer Conference in San Francisco and earned a standing ovation. He and his group developed the mouse, split-screen windows, and other innovations that subsequently became part of the office automation and personal computer revolution.

Engelbart joined Tymshare, Inc., as a senior scientist in 1977 and now has that position at McDonnell Douglas Corporation. Not easily diverted from his crusade, Engelbart feels that the world still has not perceived the primary potential for high-performance human augmentation.

DOUG ENGELBART

Winding through the well-groomed streets of Atherton, at last I found Doug Engelbart's home, tucked away in a grove of redwoods and oaks. I wondered if I would see any evidence of the fire that had burned his home eight years before.

A pleasant, scholarly man, Engelbart met me at the door of his rebuilt home. He took me into the kitchen-dining area, where we sat at a table and talked about his early days at SRI as well as his recent concern about nuclear war. His wife, Ballard, joined us after a few minutes and served a light late-afternoon snack of cold drinks and small, home-baked quiches. As he followed me outside to find some locations for his portrait I glanced back and saw him emerging from the kitchen door with his daughter's dog, Tasha. The contrast of Engelbart's white hair against the dark background looked good. Luckily, he had a few dog biscuits tucked away in his pockets for Tasha's curiosity and reward. Making this portrait defied my Puritan ethic: it was almost too easy.

Edward A. Feigenbaum

Edward Feigenbaum's work at Stanford University began the application of artificial intelligence to practical problems, moving the computer world into the "fifth generation." The first four generations were based on hardware—the vacuum tube, transistor, integrated circuit, and very large scale integrated circuit. The fifth generation is defined by function—the computer with artificial intelligence (AI) that reasons with knowledge. Feigenbaum says this is "not only the second computer revolution, but the important one." He and Pamela McCorduck, in their recent book on this new trend, state that if the United States doesn't rise to the challenge of Japan's fifth generation computer project, our nation may be consigned to the role of the first great postindustrial agrarian society.

Born in 1936 in Weehawken, New Jersey, Feigenbaum's brilliance in the field of computers first surfaced at Carnegie Mellon University, where he earned a B.S. in electrical engineering and a Ph.D. in industrial administration in 1960. Feigenbaum reflected on his study with Herbert Simon and Allen Newell, saying, "I was fortunate to be at the right place at the right time to take this exciting intellectual voyage."

A Fulbright scholarship took Feigenbaum to England. He returned to a professorship at U.C. Berkeley and then moved to Stanford when he was twenty-nine. At Stanford he worked with Nobel laureate Joshua Lederberg and Bruce Buchanan to create the Heuristic Programming Project, a laboratory that does basic research on expert system programs to perform complex reasoning tasks at levels equalling or exceeding human competence. Feigenbaum has helped to found two startup companies, Teknowledge and IntelliCorp. He foresees intelligent computers as amplifiers of our own intelligence and believes "they will profoundly affect our businesses and professions, our institutions and our governments, our science, our schools, and our personal daily lives."

In 1986 he was awarded membership in the National Academy of Engineering "for pioneering contributions to knowledge engineering and expert systems technology."

Feigenbaum is consumed by his work, devoting his life to the discovery of knowledge that he says "is power, and computers that amplify that knowledge will amplify every dimension of power."

EDWARD A. FEIGENBAUM

We had plenty to talk about. Feigenbaum's Japanese-born wife, Penny Nii, had recently coauthored *The First Artificial Intelligence Coloring Book*, so that was a perfect opener.

Because I wanted his pipe in the photograph, I asked him to light it. As he did, he told me about Palo Alto's new ordinance to ban smoking in offices, which would prevent his pipe smoking and might, he said, "disrupt my thinking." God forbid that this man's thinking be disrupted. This warrants a variance.

I wanted to photograph Feigenbaum near a window with light streaming in through slatted blinds and with his wife's photograph in the background. Then he suggested a corner with a blackboard and the American Library Association's poster depicting a genie tornadoing up from an open book. Feigenbaum said, "This is about the work I do." The poster was captioned "Knowledge Is Real Power."

Kenneth E. Haughton

Born in 1928, Kenneth E. Haughton planned to be a logger like his father. His first job in an Oregon lumber camp paid him as much as his father was earning after a lifetime in the woods, and Haughton recalls thinking, "This is crazy. There is no future here and I'd better do something about it." His parents couldn't afford college for their son, so he joined the Marine Corps. From 1946 to 1948 he was stationed in San Francisco and worked as a watch repairman. He met his wife Beverly during those years, liked the area, and decided to stay in California.

Using the GI Bill to finance his schooling, Haughton enrolled at the University of California at Berkeley. In choosing a major he was torn between teaching and engineering but chose the latter, reasoning that as a practicing engineer he could also teach. He earned a bachelor's degree in mechanical engineering, then attended Iowa State College for a master's degree before returning to Berkeley to earn a Ph.D. His teaching assignments have included Iowa State, Cornell, and, since 1982, the University of Santa Clara, where he is presently dean of the school of engineering.

During twenty-five years with IBM, Haughton made many key contributions to the development of magnetic disk storage. One effort, though, is particularly well known. In the early 1970s he headed the team that produced the Winchester disk drive, incorporating a major advance in the magnetic head structure that "reads" the information on a disk. The name Winchester was given to the drive by the engineering group because it had two storage units, each capable of holding thirty megabytes of data. The combination became known as the thirty-thirty, which is also a nickname for the famous Winchester 30-30 caliber rifle. This advance in data storage had a dramatic effect in improving computer performance. *Winchester* is now a household word in the industry.

By avocation, Haughton is a genealogist who spends hours researching his family history. A fisherman as well, he claims there is never enough time for fishing mountain streams. He is also a world traveler whose favorite haunts include New Zealand, China, and eastern Europe.

KENNETH E. HAUGHTON

Lugging my equipment up to the second floor of the engineering building at the University of Santa Clara on an unusually hot day was no fun. But when I arrived my mood changed. Haughton was a pleasant man who ushered me into his office and introduced me to Dr. Ma, a visiting friend who formerly worked for IBM. They invited me to sit down and chat before making the portrait. In academia there seems to be a more relaxed pace than I found in business offices. We three talked for fifteen minutes before I opened my camera bag.

I asked Haughton where he might like me to photograph him. He showed me an old typewriter on which someone had rigged up a disk as a gag gift when he left the Lexington, Kentucky, IBM lab to come to San Jose. He was obviously proud of this memento. We discussed photographs of his children, then talked more about his work on the Winchester disk drive. He enjoyed telling the story of how it got its name from the rifle. Haughton seemed like a thoughtful, kind man who was doing just what he wanted to do with his life.

steven jobs

S

teven Paul Jobs, the cofounder of Apple Computer with Steve Wozniak, is the Johnny Appleseed of personal computers. A man of many dreams, he hopes to change the world with computers.

Jobs grew up in a middle-class family in Mountain View and Los Altos, towns within Silicon Valley. When he was fourteen years old he met Wozniak through a mutual friend and says, "Woz was the first person I met who knew more about electronics than I did." At Reed College in Oregon he studied physics, literature, and poetry, but left before graduating.

He went to work at Atari and renewed his friendship with Wozniak. The two designed computer games and attended Homebrew Computer Club meetings. When Jobs recognized the great promise in Woz's designs, he decided they should go into business. Work began in the Jobs's family garage. "The Byte Shop in Mountain View bought fifty fully assembled computers," recalls Jobs, "the biggest single episode in all of the company's history." He gave the new company its name, linking one of his favorite fruits with a play on the computer term *byte*.

Jobs has a master's eye for quality, a silver tongue, and an almost religious faith in his own intuition. In his drive for excellence he exhibits remarkable patience and persistence in making something better. He is also described as stubborn, outspoken, aggressive, and audacious.

Throughout Apple's unprecedented expansion, Jobs functioned as the company dynamo and personality. By his twenty-fifth birthday in 1980 he was worth over $100 million. By his thirtieth, Steven Jobs had left Apple to start another computer company which will make computers for colleges. His new company is appropriately called NEXT.

STEVEN JOBS

After two "lost" letters, dozens of phone calls, uncounted postcards, two broken appointments, a half-hour meeting so Jobs could check me out, and eighteen months, I finally got to photograph Steve Jobs. And by the end of the session I even liked the guy.

"Jobs hates having his picture taken," his assistant had told me. He had requested the sitting on the Stanford campus, so we tried several pillars and walls, and gradually he loosened up. As I took a meter reading I mentioned Ansel Adams. "I had an appointment to meet him, and he died three days before my trip to his Carmel home. I was really disappointed. I have a lot of his photographs." I knew Jobs likes black-and-white photography because Apple's recent annual report was in black and white—an unusual example of Jobs's sophisticated touch.

Finished with the photographs, we sat on a sandstone wall and talked about business ethics. I told him I'd had a discussion the evening before with a venture capitalist about the ethics of company defectors. Jobs said, "It was so-called defections that helped build Silicon Valley. For example, the guys who left Shockley to start Fairchild, then left Fairchild to start Intel."

After an hour and a half, Jobs was less melancholy and more animated. We talked about several subjects: the title of this book, his parents, his new I.M. Pei "closet" in New York City, the mouse for the Macintosh computer, and politics. I found Jobs the most camera-shy person and the most contentious person I've ever photographed. He loved the repartee, the one-upmanship. And I loved baiting him. I asked him, "Why do some people want only the best? Why can't they be content wanting just 'good'?" Jobs replied, "We get to create only a few things in this life. We really have such a short time here, some of us just want to make it count."

Reynold B. Johnson (signature)

Every American student taking a standardized test since 1937 has come in contact with Rey Johnson's first major invention or one of its derivatives. In 1931 he developed an electric test-score machine to expedite grading the papers of his high-school science and math students. IBM bought the invention and commercialized it, and as a result, generations of students have marked little boxes.

The magnetic disk was also Johnson's creation, the technological milestone that made stored information directly and rapidly available for computer processing. These storage platters are a part of nearly every computer system. Airline reservation systems, inventory management, automated banking, space flights, word processing, and personal computing became realities because of this advance.

Johnson's IBM-San Jose team developed the magnetic disk in 1955 for the RAMAC (Random Access Method of Accounting and Control) computer. Louis D. Stevens, who headed that program, says, "Rey Johnson had some sort of magical combination of personal creativity and unorthodox management techniques." On the day their product was unveiled, IBM President Thomas J. Watson, Jr., said, "Today is the greatest product day in the history of IBM and, I believe, in the history of the office equipment industry."

Johnson grew up on the Minnesota farm where he was born in 1906. After graduation from the University of Minnesota, he taught science and math at a Michigan high school, where he developed his scoring machine.

While at IBM between 1934 and 1971, Johnson was granted eighty-four patents, many of which were fundamental to IBM's technological preeminence. After retiring from IBM, Johnson founded the Education Engineering Associates Laboratory in Palo Alto, where he has developed many more inventions. Johnson was awarded the National Medal of Technology by President Reagan in 1986. In a play on the word *world* and because of the whirl of projects underway, Johnson and his wife, Beatrice, call the office behind their home the Whirled Headquarters of Educational Engineering.

R E Y N O L D   B .   J O H N S O N

It was evident when I walked into their backyard cottage office that this couple had been together a long time, relied on each other, and liked each other. When I asked about their backgrounds, I learned they met when both taught high school. Rey Johnson was developing his scoring machine; Beatrice Rashleigh wrote an article about it for the local newspaper. Her story was sent out over the Associated Press wire, and Edward R. Murrow picked it up for radio. Next IBM heard about it, eventually bought the machine, and hired Johnson. Rashleigh became Johnson's wife and, as he asserts, "Still is!"

Johnson was British-proper without being British. Although modest, he told me about his patents with great pride. He chuckled as he picked up one of his teaching inventions, a birdsong machine, saying, "This would be a great device to teach people languages. We'd have to change the recording, of course."

Beatrice Johnson offered me assistance, then retreated to her computer in the corner of the office. Occasionally Johnson would softly ask her where something was or when something happened. I liked watching the interaction of two people who are together twenty-four hours a day and obviously enjoy it.

*F*ather of the personal computer" is a title Alan Kay disclaims. But many people insist that Kay's ideas succeeded in getting industry's attention for the personal computer.

Much of this attention resulted from research done at the Xerox Palo Alto Research Center (PARC). The Golden Age of PARC occurred between 1971 and 1976, when Xerox gave a blank check to a group of young and talented computer scientists in a creative think-tank environment. Here Kay conceived of Dynabook, the powerful notebook-size personal computer. Dynabook inspired Alto, the forerunner of Apple's Macintosh. Another celebrated Kay contribution was Smalltalk, a high-level, object-oriented programming language used by nonprogrammers. He also pioneered the use of icons (look-alike symbols) instead of typed words for telling computers what to do next.

Pledging never to design a personal computer that couldn't be used by a child, Kay explains, "I think that since children appear to have to construct the world inside their heads in order to become human beings, then people must be natural constructors. Computers are the best construction material we have ever come up with outside of our own brains."

Kay, whose father was a physiology professor and artist/musician, grew up in Massachusetts and New York. He received a bachelor's degree in mathematics and molecular biology from the University of Colorado in 1966. After earning a Ph.D. in computer science at the University of Utah in 1969, he joined the artificial intelligence project at Stanford. He is presently an Apple Fellow, one of three select scientists who pursue "far-out ideas" for Apple Computer's future.

Kay dismisses concerns that artificial intelligence will lead to the takeover of the world by computers. "Some people worry that artificial intelligence will make us feel inferior, but then, anybody in his right mind should have an inferiority complex every time he looks at a flower!"

A L A N   K A Y

While I waited for him, I had a chance to wander around the Macintosh building looking for a spot in which to photograph this computer whiz kid. A friend had told me earlier that morning that Kay plays the piano, so what better place than at the new Bösendorfer in the Apple employee lounge.

Kay looked like a teenager walking across the Apple Computer parking lot: corduroy pants, polo shirt, and a radio on his hip. He was smiling and seemingly at ease with the world. I told him I wanted to use the piano in the portrait, so he walked over, sat down, and started playing. This was one of my favorite experiences while putting together the book. The music was so beautiful that a number of hard-working Apple people emerged from their offices to listen. I later learned that he had been improvising.

Donald Knuth (signature)

Donald Knuth stayed home from the eighth grade for two weeks to enter a contest. By making 4500 words from the letters in the name *Ziegler's Giant Bar,* he won candy bars for everyone in his class and a television set for his school. His early fascination with words has continued. A list of Knuth's publications, which cover a variety of topics, is eleven pages long.

Knuth attended Lutheran schools in Milwaukee, where he was born in 1938. He relished both music and physics in high school, but physics won the career toss because of the college scholarship offered him. Knuth graduated from Case Institute of Technology summa cum laude and received an unprecedented simultaneous M.S. degree for his work.

Computers entered Knuth's life between his freshman and sophomore years in college, and he was hooked. After receiving a Ph.D. from California Institute of Technology in 1963, Knuth joined their faculty. In 1968 he came to Stanford, where he is currently professor of computer science.

Concerned about the education system in the United States, he finds math textbooks disappointing. "There is too much emphasis on flashy things and on memorizing formulas," he says. This interest led to his writing the widely acclaimed textbook *The Art of Computer Programming,* a project he began in 1962. Knuth anticipates a seven-volume series. Three are complete. He keeps notebooks to schedule his time but often wakes up saying, "Another day and the book isn't finished."

Proof that he can work at a different pace is his book *Surreal Numbers,* which was completed in one week. Knuth's thoughts came so fast he could only write the first letter of every word. Then, the day after, he had to figure out what he had meant to say.

Knuth says, "I sometimes consider myself a pure mathematician, but usually I'm a pure computer scientist who has found connections between computers and mathematics."

DONALD KNUTH

Knuth's contemporary home of natural wood stood out on its Stanford campus street. The yard and entry were fastidiously neat. A towering man opened the door, smiled shyly, and invited me in.

I wanted to photograph him at the pipe organ that dominates the livingroom, and as I set up my camera he played a prelude and fugue by Bach. I forgot to photograph him playing—until he finished. What beautiful lines in that musical instrument so perfectly attuned to his mathematical mind! Every section of the organ offered the sort of graphic background or abstraction that photographers dream about. He told me he had helped design it. One of his musical goals is to write an organ compositon based on the Biblical book of Revelation, making the musical themes correspond to the symbolism of the book.

I asked Knuth a few questions about his life. He told me that his mother, visiting him while recovering from foot surgery at nearby Stanford Hospital, might tell me about his childhood. He hung around while I quizzed her about her precocious son. She said that Knuth learned to read by associating the letters from stories his parents read him with the letters on a Hills Brothers coffee carton she used for carrying her groceries home. I mentioned how some mothers hold flash cards in front of their babies, trying to teach them to read. Mrs. Knuth said, "That's something I never had to worry about. My biggest problem when Don was a small boy was convincing the public library to accept him in their school-age group of advanced readers called The Bookworms even though he was just three years old."

Sandra L. Kurtzig

Sandra Lynn Kurtzig founded ASK Computer Systems on a $2000 shoestring and turned it into an $80 million company in ten years. She is the only woman to found and direct a publicly owned high-technology company in Silicon Valley.

Born in Chicago in 1946, Kurtzig moved to Los Angeles with her family when she was eleven. Her background offers few clues that would foreshadow her later success in the computer industry. Her father made his living as a real-estate developer and her mother as a writer.

Kurtzig's interest in science flourished at the University of California at Los Angeles, where she received a B.A. in chemistry and math. She then came to Stanford to earn a master's in aeronautical engineering. After holding technical and marketing positions with General Electric and TRW, she left full-time employment to raise her two sons while writing software part time.

In 1973 Kurtzig introduced the result of that home software work: a minicomputer-based management information system for manufacturing companies. ASK programs are designed to improve inventory control and financial and production management. "When I first started ASK," she says, "I'd go to parties and tell people I was in software. They usually thought I made women's underwear!"

ASK was named Growth Company of the Year in 1984 by the Association for Corporate Growth. Kurtzig lists four prerequisites for being a successful entrepreneur: "Believe in yourself, hire good people, set realistic goals, and work long and hard."

In mid-1985 Kurtzig relinquished her daily responsibilities at ASK but has remained involved in the company's long-range planning. Reflecting upon her success, Kurtzig says, "The most important thing for me was just having the guts to get started. Everybody has good ideas, but unless you get out there and research your idea and its market, you never know what you could have done. I've been surprising myself every step of the way."

SANDRA L. KURTZIG

Because she's the only woman in the book, I wanted Sandy Kurtzig's portrait to be exceptionally good. She let me try three times. First I photographed her at her desk in her glamorous home in the hills of Atherton. Next we tried her spacious office at ASK. I finally got the portrait back at her home as she sat in her comfortable bedroom armchair.

Intense, quick, and witty, this high-powered woman nonetheless made it clear that she hasn't lost touch with regular people. She goes to the most elegant parties in Silicon Valley, but she continues to enjoy interaction with noncelebrities, too. When I arrived at her home in my Levi's to make her portrait, she invited me in to meet her date and share a bottle of California champagne.

Kurtzig cooperated, encouraged me, and gave me confidence. She let me see the personality that has brought success to her and her company.

Robert R. Maxfield

M

any consider Robert Maxfield, the "M" founder of ROLM Corporation, the genius behind its research and development. He disagrees. "I'm good at stimulating ideas from others, then figuring out which are the best ones and making them happen."

Born in Detroit in 1941, Maxfield grew up in Wichita Falls, Texas, where his father was an orthopedic surgeon. He competed in high-school and college swim meets, winning two state championship gold medals and setting a state record in the individual medley.

Maxfield knew he wanted to major in science or engineering at Rice University and narrowed the choice this way: "My sophomore year I took chemistry and the lab seemed like a lot of dishwashing, so I eliminated that. Then I tried to decide between electrical and mechanical engineering. I knew that if I majored in mechanical engineering, I would learn how to work on my car. If I majored in electrical, I could build my own stereo. I chose the latter."

Maxfield received a B.S.E.E. in 1964. Then, while working as an engineer at IBM in San Jose, he earned his master's and Ph.D. in electrical engineering at Stanford. In 1969 he became one of the four cofounders of ROLM Corporation, a manufacturer of business communication systems and military computers. Widely regarded as the key technical and operations figure behind ROLM's phenomenal success, Maxfield served as executive vice-president and as a member of its board of directors. Upon ROLM's acquisition by IBM in 1984, Maxfield once again found himself working for "Big Blue."

When Maxfield and his family have opportunities to travel, they like to go where they can study archaeological ruins such as those of the Greek and Mayan civilizations. With no hesitation, he admits he's a workaholic who enjoys setting goals and achieving them.

ROBERT R. MAXFIELD

I first heard of Bobby Maxfield in the early 1960s when he and his wife Melinda participated in car rallies with mutual friends. Next thing I knew, this man had helped start a company and moved to a bigger house, but little else had changed. He still enjoys cars (he has a classic Mercedes 300 "gull wing" coupe and took Bob Bondurant's famous race-car driving class), and he swims every day. But now he only has to go to his backyard for the swim or to the pool that ROLM constructed for its employees at the campuslike corporate facilities in Santa Clara.

Maxfield fits his Southern nickname, Bobby. Boyish-looking in his early forties, he resembles a teenager I sat behind in algebra class in Texas. And he seems as reserved as a studious undergraduate. As we toured his remodeled sixty-year-old home in Saratoga, we discussed Rice, our mutual alma mater. He laughed embarrassedly when I mentioned that several people call him the Silicon Valley king of the game Trivial Pursuit. I reminded him that he's the only person I know who got the answer to the question, "What are scientists looking for in several tons of cleaning fluid in an underground chamber?"(answer: neutrinos).

As we talked in his lush and inviting family room, he relaxed on a new chintz-covered sofa. I made a few photographs there. Then Maxfield, always a good sport, consented to photographs in his swimming pool. He got into the water, squinted with the sun in his eyes, and let me take pictures. He swam, got his hair wet, and I kept photographing. Then he put on his goggles, looked silly, and let me continue. Bobby Maxfield is unhampered by vanity.

John McCarthy

While teaching at Dartmouth College in 1955, John McCarthy coined the term *artificial intelligence* to describe the programming of computers to perform learning and reasoning functions. A pioneer of computer science, he invented time sharing and developed the LISP programming language, a system for computing with symbolic expressions. He continues to contribute broadly to the foundations of AI.

McCarthy was born in Boston in 1927. His father was a carpenter and trade-union organizer. His mother was a journalist and social worker. Always interested in math, McCarthy majored in that subject at California Institute of Technology, receiving a B.S. in 1948. Three years later he earned a Ph.D. in mathematics at Princeton.

In 1962 McCarthy came to Stanford University as full professor of computer science. From 1965 to 1980 he organized and served as director of the Artificial Intelligence Laboratory on campus. A member of the American Academy of Arts and Sciences, he also serves on the board of directors of a company that is involved in commercializing AI.

McCarthy's LISP programming language, invented in 1960, has recently become even more prominent. Several companies are making specialized LISP computers, and the Defense Department has adopted common LISP as one of its two standard programming languages. Much of his recent research has concerned the formalization of nonmonotonic reasoning in an effort to make computers "reason" in ways more like those of human beings. McCarthy feels optimistic about the prospects for progress in that direction. In a 1982 article on Silicon Valley in *National Geographic* McCarthy is quoted as saying, "There's no reason we can't build machines that think."

JOHN McCARTHY

McCarthy's Stanford office is a scientific library. That room held more books than any other office I visited. File cabinets bulged. The entire chamber brimmed with information. The only thing that felt familiar was a photograph—and that was of a rocket.

McCarthy walked into his office after teaching a class. He was quiet, not eager to be photographed except that he needed a photograph for his private use. I was fascinated by his deep-set eyes under a heavy shock of white hair. His expression changed rapidly as we talked. One minute he looked like a gravely intellec-tual middle-aged man and the next, a bemused young boy smiling happily at the world. I liked the range. It gave him an enigmatic quality.

As we briefly discussed computer science, a student peered in and asked him a question. McCarthy seemed embarrassed to be seen being photographed and apologized, saying he'd be out in just a minute. I hurried, packed up, and left. I was sorry we didn't have time to talk more about his work, his support of the "Star Wars" defense program, and how he hit upon the name artificial intelligence. Enigmatic he will remain.

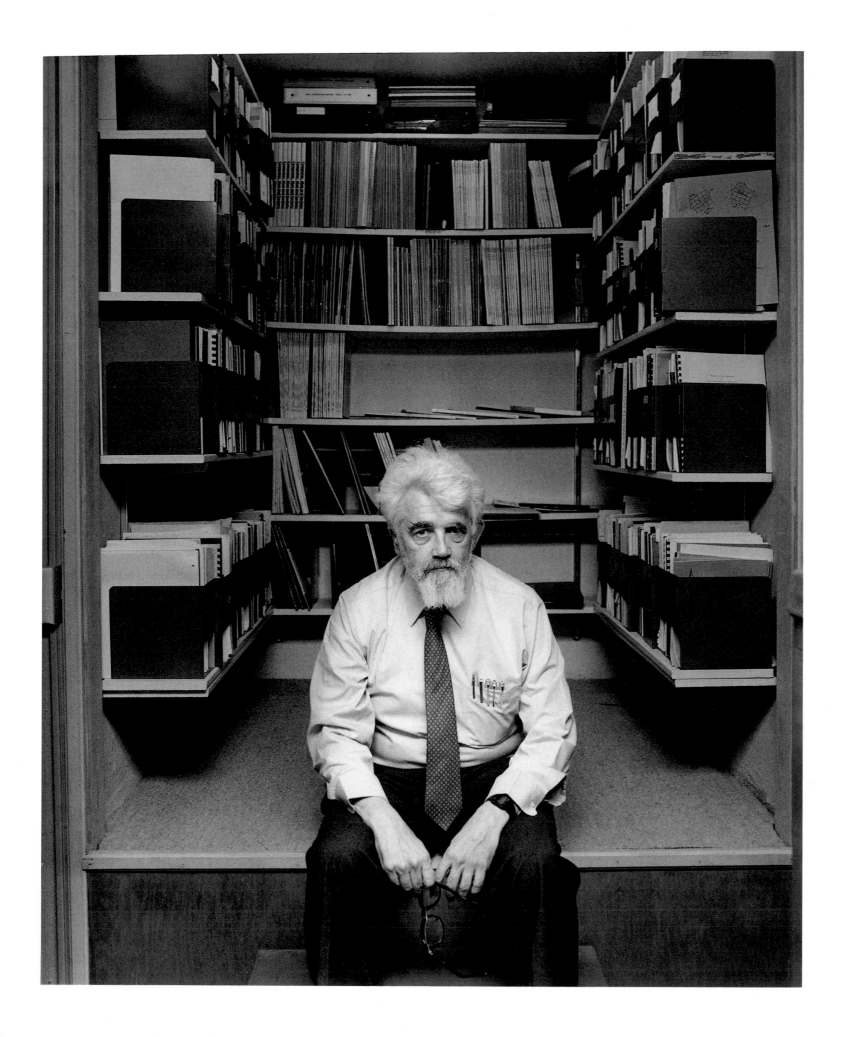

Adam Osborne

Adam Osborne, an industry guru and master of hype, was born in Thailand and spent his childhood in India. His father was a countermissionary who tried to convert Christians to Hinduism. Sent to England for high school, Osborne aquired his basic philosophy: "If there is something you really want, you should go for it."

He ran a bookie operation while attending the University of Birmingham in England. Covering most of the bets himself, he worked his way through one term of school—until his luck changed.

After receiving his doctorate in chemical engineering in 1968, Osborne worked for Shell Development Corporation. "I was bored, didn't do well, and got fired," he recalls. He then started his own technical writing company. His computer magazine column, "From the Fountainhead," earned him a reputation as the Howard Cosell of the personal computer industry.

Proceeds from the sale of his publishing company to McGraw-Hill in 1979 provided him with funds to move on to his next venture, building the first portable computer. The twenty-four-pound Osborne 1 sold at the then-lowest price in the industry. Osborne pushed his product and company to $100 million sales in one year. A short-lived success, Osborne Computer announced bankruptcy in September 1983, from which it emerged (without him) in early 1985.

Osborne has since started a new software firm, Paperback Software International, which markets a line of productivity and educational programs via bookshops, software stores, and computer stores. He hopes to reshape the software industry by drastically lowering microcomputer software prices.

Many see the man as "sometimes brilliant, sometimes eccentric, and always outspoken." He is also described as self-confident, enthusiastic, and energetic. Osborne himself claims others view him as "either a visionary or an obnoxious jerk."

A D A M   O S B O R N E

My trip to the Berkeley hills was rewarded with a cup of espresso made from freshly ground beans by Osborne in his large kitchen. Influenced by what I'd read about him, I suppose I'd expected a growling terror. Instead I was met with a pleasant smile and a soft-spoken voice with an English accent, in an airy redwood house with skylights, art, and a view. To top it off, Osborne owns and loves cats: IMSAI joined us during the photographing session, whereupon I was told he got his name from a major computer manufacturer. But P.C. didn't show up. It was obvious what that name meant, so obvious that Osborne corrected me: Party Cat.

When I expressed surprise that he seemed gentler than the man newspaper and magazine articles had depicted as brash, Osborne said, "That's probably because, when I go to meetings and invite questions, I give them honest answers. I am very direct. Some people may interpret that as brutal or arrogant."

We continued a polite conversation about his interest in rock music, his favorite book of the past few years, *Endless Enemies*, and the art he and his wife, Barbara Burdick, collect, which includes a photograph by Matthew Naythons.

Once during our photographing session, Osborne abruptly excused himself to call his secretary with a question. I realized that this is a double-track person who never stops working in his head even while carrying on a conversation.

M Kenneth Oshman (signature)

Malin Kenneth Oshman learned the realities of the marketplace as a teenage cotton broker dealing with the shrewd farmers around Rosenberg, Texas. As cofounder in 1969 and president of ROLM Corporation, he began his telecommunications and computer business in a prune shed in Cupertino. Fifteen years later, he negotiated the sale of ROLM to IBM for more than $1 billion.

A high-school friend, Houston physician Charles ("Bubba") Yates, says Ken Oshman exhibited his business acumen early by foiling an "impossible" biology teacher who passed out a sheet of "impossible" questions for a study guide, warning that the final exam would be based on the study guide and that failure was a certainty without the answers. Oshman organized the FONY note company, named for three classmates and himself. The young business partners researched the answers to the study guide and sold them to every biology student in the school.

While at Rice University, Oshman played the stock market, lost most of his summer earnings, and learned an important lesson: "The only way to make money in stocks is to invest in good companies and managements and forget about short-term market and company fluctuations."

He received B.A. and B.S.E.E. degrees from Rice, where professors said they were never able to challenge him sufficiently. He married his childhood sweetheart, Barbara Daily, and in 1963 was recruited by Burton McMurtry to join Sylvania in Mountain View. He worked as an engineer and simultaneously attended Stanford on the Honors Co-op program, earning an M.S. and a Ph.D. in electrical engineering in record time. Oshman had a short but productive career as a researcher in lasers and nonlinear optics. With backing from venture capitalist Jack Melchor, Oshman and three other Rice graduates (Gene Richeson, Walter Loewenstern, and Robert Maxfield) founded ROLM, an acronym consisting of their initials.

Widely regarded as a person who takes command, Oshman is competitive, magnetic, and energetic. Leo Chamberlain, a retired ROLM executive vice-president, describes Oshman as "a man who challenges the thoroughness of your thinking. Ken is a brilliant business person who absorbs a tremendous amount of information, throws away the junk, and keeps the kernel."

M. KENNETH OSHMAN

The Oshmans' new home in an affluent Peninsula town displayed my idea of good taste—simple lines typical of Goodwin Steinberg's architecture. I enjoyed being greeted by the modern sculpture in the atrium and in the garden.

Because I like the feeling of natural or existing light in portraits, I try to find locations where the subject looks good and feels relaxed. I had no trouble finding places in the Oshmans' house. They had directed Steinberg to "give enough light to read by in every sitting area." As Oshman showed me around, I gravitated to his study, where he had been listening to the Saturday afternoon ballgame while working on a stack of papers. That room felt like his private retreat.

Friendly, sensitive, and completely cooperative, Oshman let me photograph him sitting behind his desk, in front of a new monotype print, and perching on a countertop of his custom-crafted oak cabinets. He was comfortable in front of my camera. When I told him I needed some variety in the book and wanted a portrait of someone in a hat, he took me to his closet and pulled out three great ones. We went outside, he tried each one on while puffing on his cigar, and I clicked away. He seemed unpressured and let me take as long as I needed. Several times he said, "Do what you want. You're the artist." I feel that this attitude brings out the best in people—something he has achieved over and over during his rapid rise to the top.

Alan F. Shugart (signature)

Money," Alan Shugart says bluntly. "That's my motivation." Born in Los Angeles in 1930, he attended the University of Redlands on a scholarship, receiving a B.S. degree in engineering and physics in 1951.

At IBM-San Jose, Shugart was in charge of all disk-drive development during the time the floppy disk was invented there. When he moved to Memorex in 1969, he took with him a number of key engineers who pushed that company into the ranks of successful manufacturers of IBM-compatible equipment. By 1973 Memorex was in financial trouble, and Shugart decided to start Shugart Associates, one of the first firms to offer floppy disk drives to original equipment manufacturer (OEM) systems designers. The firm developed and manufactured the first eight-inch floppy disks, but money ran low and Shugart left under pressure. He spent some time as a commercial fisherman and part-time business consultant, then found backing for a new disk-drive venture, Seagate Technology. Within three years, the company moved from startup to industry leader. Shugart is chief executive officer and chairman of the board.

Roger Smith, president of Silicon Valley Bank, says: "Shugart has the tenacity of a bulldog, a general knowledge of the total computer field, and the ability to look forward and create new products. While he tends to be blunt and direct, underneath is a big-hearted man who tries to help others be successful in building their own companies."

ALAN F. SHUGART

There was something challenging about Alan Shugart. He was the only person who refused outright to be featured in the book, saying he didn't "need the notoriety." But after three letters and as many phone calls, he conceded with a gruff, "OK. I'll let you take my picture." A few weeks later I drove over the Santa Cruz Mountains to Scotts Valley for the portrait. As I walked into Shugart's office, with a teasing smile he barked, "You're late!" Fifteen years ago I would have withered and probably cried. Now I was more confident. "No, I'm not late," I said. "I've been waiting in your lobby five minutes!"

With the air cleared, we began the session at his desk. Native redwood trees outside his window provided a good background. Then we migrated to the hallway where I had seen Alan Ross's photographs. I thought that if the man liked this kind of black-and-white photography, he did indeed have a sensitive side—and good taste. He told me about commissioning Ross to take annual report photographs, which he liked so much that he arranged for Seagate to exhibit them. The company subsequently bought the entire show for the lobby and hallways.

I thought we really had *the* portrait in the picture of Shugart standing in his hallway amid the photographs, but I hadn't spent much time and felt Shugart might feel cheated because he'd set aside thirty minutes for the sitting. So we went out to the front of the building to make a few more. As we walked out, I told him I'd read that his wife, Rita, had bought a new red Ferrari. He laughingly replied, "Yes, I call her 'the ultimate consumer.'" We chatted about that car as the symbol of the people around here who have "made it," agreeing that the car had to be red. Anything other than Italy's racing color just wouldn't be right for a Ferrari in Silicon Valley.

James G. Treybig (signature)

Eleven years after James Treybig founded Tandem Computers, Inc., it made the *Fortune* 500 list. The company now has more than 5000 employees and annual revenues of over half a billion dollars.

The innovation that caused this growth was Tandem's NonStop on-line transaction processing computers, systems structured to offer uninterrupted operation in the face of malfunctions. This eliminates the costly computer downtime that plagues more conventional systems. Banks, airlines, and newspapers, critically dependent upon keeping their computers running even while repairs are being made, are among Tandem's customers.

The company is also innovative in its attitude and concern for employees, receiving much publicity for its Friday-afternoon popcorn parties and conspicuously accessible top management. "You've got to stay close to your employees and make them feel they're important, that the company cares," Treybig says.

Born in 1940 in the Texas panhandle where his father was a geophysicist, Treybig received a B.A. and a B.S.E.E. from Rice University. He decided on a business career when he took over as manager of the yearbook and made a profit. After earning his M.B.A. from Stanford, he worked for Texas Instruments and Hewlett-Packard and then joined the venture capital firm of Kleiner, Perkins, Caulfield, and Byers. While there he recognized the need for computers that don't break down and developed the plan that in 1974 resulted in Tandem.

Outgoing, informal, and with a disarming country-boy manner, Treybig has maintained his deep Texas accent through twenty years of California residency. Everybody who knows him calls him Jimmy T.

JAMES G. TREYBIG

Treybig has been interested in radios ever since his teens. His Los Altos Hills home is evidence that the interest hasn't waned.

"Yew kin spot mah house way bafor yew git there. Mah roof is loaded with an-tennahs." I had forgotten what Texans from the Panhandle sound like, but Jimmy Treybig's drawl reminded me. Shore 'nough, those antennas directed me to his hillside home. Treybig met me in the driveway and invited me through the open garage into his kitchen. We sat at his breakfast table, which was covered with the Sunday newspapers. As we drank Dr. Pepper we discussed Silicon Valley companies and the people who had built the area's electronics industry.

Looking for a place to make the portrait, Treybig said, "Wanna see mah radio room?" We lugged my equipment upstairs to a small room adjoining the enormous master bedroom. Treybig began going through the motions of tidying up, which was impossible in that workroom with its tools, tubes, parts, and wires. I felt that this room is where the man's soul is. He pointed behind his radios to the wall covered with postcards from ham operators he's communicated with. "Ah've bin all over th' worl' to ham radio stations, to places ah'd never dreamed ah wud see. Ah've bin to Greenland, Gambia, Easter Island, and Belize."

I was thrilled to be in this room, to feel some of the excitement he must experience when he communicates with the voices from far away—on machines he built himself. He was the living key to something that baffles me: radio. Aside from his business victories, Jimmy Treybig had conquered the invisible riddles of radio waves, and I was happy he let me into that world—temporarily.

Woz

Stephan Wozniak is the "wizard" who designed the original products for the company he cofounded, Apple Computer. Born in 1950, he grew up in the heart of Silicon Valley, where his father is an engineer at Lockheed Missiles and Space Company and his mother is involved in theatre and politics. Woz built his first computer when he was thirteen and took top prizes in a science fair. At nineteen he met fourteen-year-old Steve Jobs. The two teenagers built an electronic "blue box" enabling them to make free toll calls by seizing phone-company lines. The young entrepreneurs sold 200 boxes to fellow students at eighty dollars each.

While he was at Hewlett-Packard, Wozniak was a member of the Homebrew Computer Club, to which Jobs also belonged. Woz's involvement resulted in the Apple I design. When Jobs got orders for fifty of the machines from the Byte Shop in Mountain View in 1976, Apple Computer, Inc.—and with it the home computer industry—was born.

By 1977 Wozniak had accomplished what he considers his most important work, the design of the Apple II, and Apple began its incredible growth surge. But Wozniak disliked meetings and memos and began to withdraw from the corporate world. A near-fatal plane crash in 1981 forced him to take time off. Under an assumed name, Wozniak went to the University of California at Berkeley where he earned a degree in computer science. In April 1985 he founded CL-9 (Cloud 9) to market a programmable remote-control video device he had designed.

Apart from his technical life, Wozniak is concerned with social issues, the world of rock music, and his friends and relatives. To offset budget cuts, he donated $50,000 to his former school district. In the early 1980s he gained attention by producing two rock festivals that lost $25 million. Wozniak has made generous donations of his Apple stock, and his name regularly appears on the sponsor lists for a wide variety of local cultural and educational activities. About all this, Wozniak says, "I'd rather be liked than be rich."

STEVE WOZNIAK

I arrived at 9:00 AM at Steve Wozniak's castlelike home in the Los Gatos hills. A man dressed in neat new Levi's, a starched shirt, and a belt with an Apple logo on the buckle stepped out of his front door. Steve Wozniak did not look like the teenage nerd I had heard him called. Nor did he look like the press photographs from Apple's beginnings. His hair was not long and straggly but Beatles-length and blown dry. The only giveaway to the original Woz was his conversational style. He answered my questions curtly, with no elaboration. "How are you?" "Fine." "Could we look around for a place you feel comfortable for the portrait?" "Yes." "May we start with your computer room?" "OK."

We reached a large room housing at least five computers, and Wozniak immediately started pushing switches and buttons. Lights popped on. He sat down at a keyboard, began typing, and said, "I'll do my banking while you set up." I had to step over and around boxes of disks and hardware on the floor, straddling some kind of machine in order to look through the lens. Woz sat back in his computer chair, not completely relaxed, and we made some pictures.

Suddenly I remembered his little boy and asked if I might photograph them together. The proud father answered me for the first time with animation, "Yes! But you'll have to wait until he wakes up—any time now." Shortly thereafter, Woz's wife, Candi, waved at us from their son Jesse's window. Woz said, "Jesse will now pull the curtain back. He will wave, too." The curtain moved, and Woz came to life. A blond, brown-eyed, curly-haired baby boy standing in his crib on the other side of the window began waving and laughing, eliciting an identical response in the thirty-four-year-old man. A few minutes later Jesse jumped into Woz's arms, and the taciturn computer genius became a relaxed, playful father.

Thomas J. Davis, Jr.

Thomas Davis became a pioneering force in the growth of high-technology industry by embarking on a new career at an age when most people are complacently eyeing retirement. He was close to fifty when he and Arthur Rock founded one of the first venture capital partnerships.

The son of a banker, Tommy Davis was born in 1912 and brought up in Cincinnati, Ohio. He attended Harvard College and then its law school, where his favorite professor was Felix Frankfurter, the famous legal scholar and Supreme Court justice. During World War II he served in the Office of Strategic Services, the predecessor to the Central Intelligence Agency. In a San Francisco hospital, Davis recuperated from jungle diseases contracted while serving in a guerrilla unit in Burma. He liked the Bay Area and brought his family to California.

During his tenure as vice-president of Kern County Land Company, an oil, cattle, and farming firm, Davis recognized "that the most valuable things came out of people's heads." He took a course in electronics, learning that the fruits of research seemed to reach the marketplace very slowly. Curious about this problem, he consulted Frederick Terman and Edward Ginzton at Stanford University. After those meetings he persuaded Kern County Land Company to back startup Watkins-Johnson Company, founded by a professor and a physicist. With no big-company bureaucracy to fight and with good product ideas, the company moved fast and became a quick success, just as Davis had predicted.

In 1959 he launched his partnership with Arthur Rock to provide funding for new electronics firms such as Teledyne and Scientific Data Systems. Davis later founded the Mayfield Fund, which included a number of Stanford professors as partners. (He named it Mayfield for the small town at the edge of the Stanford campus that became a part of Palo Alto in the 1940s.) The Mayfield Fund has invested in such successful companies as Tandem Computers, Genentech, and Applied BioSystems.

"All those old-fashioned phrases about the value of working hard made their mark on me," says Davis. "But I remain very much convinced that my basic inclination to place the individual human being at the center of the process has been right."

TOMMY DAVIS, JR.

My meeting with Tommy Davis was pure pleasure. He was friendly, exuberant, and generous with his time. I had to wait only a few minutes, and for that brief delay he apologized. He whisked me to an office that reflected his passion for horses: a sculpture on one desktop and J. F. Herring prints from the 1850s over his Victorian sofa. He told me about his daughter who, like me, has a Hasselblad camera and has "taken up photography. She's damn good, too!"

After asking him to stand in front of an antique desk for a portrait, I had him sit on the sofa. I told him he looked very regal, and he seemed to like that. I loved his cravat, lightly striped shirt, and plaid coat. At the end of the sitting I wanted to do something for fun with his door sign. He was delighted to pose, and he peered elfishly around his Mayfield Co. sign. Davis was so lively and talkative throughout the session that I well understood his reputation for being charming.

Reid W. Dennis

Reid W. Dennis loves to fly—in the air and in the rarified atmosphere of high finance. Dennis is an enthusiastic private pilot and a venture capitalist.

His career in venture capital evolved simultaneously with his corporate employment, but Dennis made personal investments in contrast with those of his employer, in some early electronic companies. His success led him to form Institutional Venture Associates in 1974 and Institutional Venture Partners in 1980, two partnerships that have enjoyed extraordinary growth. Major investments include Collagen Corporation, Seagate Technology, and Stratus Computer.

Born in 1926, Dennis grew up in San Francisco. His grandparents played an important role in his life after his father, an engineer, died when Dennis was very young. Dennis studied engineering as an undergraduate at Stanford and later earned his M.B.A. there. He worked as a securities analyst with Fireman's Fund Insurance Company, which later merged with American Express.

Dennis claims his approach to investments is betting on the people involved. "After appraising and evaluating their experience," he says, "I decide if they really can do what they say they can do. I have a deep and abiding faith in people. To be a venture capitalist, one must be both optimistic and patient."

On business trips Dennis pilots a twin-engine turboprop plane. He also owns a classic 1946 twin-engine Grumman amphibian, which he uses on family vacation trips to Lake Tahoe, Alaska, Mexico, and Guatemala. Another interest is his extensive collection of locomotive models. His civic activities center on music: Dennis serves on the boards of both the San Francisco Symphony and the Conservatory of Music and is chairman of the San Francisco Opera. Supportive of the schools he attended, he is a trustee of The Thacher School, and in 1983 he and his wife, Peggy, funded an endowed professorship in the Stanford Department of Electrical Engineering.

Dennis recalls his grandfather's advice concerning the importance of a college degree—particularly in engineering—so that he would always "have something to fall back on." And, to this day, Dennis believes the attitudes and enthusiasm for work he learned from his grandfather help him enjoy what he is doing.

REID W. DENNIS

I knew I liked Reid Dennis when I saw a small sign on his desk that said, "I contributed to the defeat of Jesse Helms," a display of wishful thinking before the 1984 elections. It was a comfortable, unostentatious office, with a shelf of familiar lucite cubes. Inside each one is a miniature company prospectus. I had seen these mementos in the offices of most of the venture capitalists and corporate attorneys. Pictures of airplanes and a map showing his travels by private plane reinforced what I had heard about this man: he loves flying.

We talked about his trips, his plane that lands on water, and about the chair he gave Stanford University. He corrected me. "The chair my wife and I gave Stanford." Then I asked him about a recent newspaper article in which he is quoted as saying there is "too much venture money chasing too few ideas." He said the article was correct. "That makes the entire system break down. More money into marginal ideas means less quality, not to mention more time spent trying to salvage those companies."

As we made the portraits, I was relieved at Dennis's complete involvement. I was using only natural light, so he had to sit perfectly still for one second. Some people can't, or if they do, they feel uncomfortable and self-conscious. Not Dennis. He took a breath, looked directly into the camera, and didn't budge.

William H. Draper [signature]

In 1981, William Draper was appointed president and chairman of the Export-Import Bank of the United States. He joined the Reagan administration after more than twenty years as one of the pioneer West Coast venture capitalists. Still a part of the Silicon Valley scene, he was selected in 1984 by *Business Week* as one of the nation's fifty "new corporate elite." Now, in 1986, he heads the United Nations Development Program.

Draper was born in Scarsdale, New York, in 1928, the son of an investment banker. In 1950 he graduated from Yale with a triple major in history, economics, and political science. After service with the army he entered Harvard Graduate School of Business, earning an M.B.A. in 1954. Eighteen years later he returned to receive the Alumni Achievement Award.

After working at Inland Steel in Chicago, he moved to Palo Alto to join his father in Draper, Gaither and Anderson, Silicon Valley's first venture capital partnership. In 1965 Draper left DGA and founded Sutter Hill Ventures. He has participated in the creation and funding of several hundred high-technology companies and served on the boards of more than twenty.

One of Sutter Hill's big success stories involves the organization and financing of a company started by a young Chinese-American, David Lee, who designed an improved daisy-wheel printer. After six years and an investment of $2 million, Qume Corporation, as it was known, was sold to ITT Corporation for $150 million. "Today," says Draper, "most of the world's word processors use a Qume printer."

In his role at the Export-Import Bank, Draper was responsible for the United States's financial export assistance activities. An ardent free-trade advocate, he has used the Bank's resources to counter subsidized financing by foreign governments and to assume risks in developing countries that private lenders are unwilling to take.

When asked about the plethora of venture capitalists in this country, Draper says, "The more, the merrier! The more venture capitalists, the more creativity will be encouraged, and the more ideas will be developed."

WILLIAM H. DRAPER III

Draper appeared at the door of his Atherton hilltop home in a swimsuit, with a beach towel around his neck. His daughter, Becky, and his new son-in-law, Geoff Mulligan, accompanied us and added fun to the photographing session. After I showed them the picture of Jerry Sanders sitting on his bed, they encouraged Draper not to change clothes for his photograph. I joined in the pleas for a swimsuit portrait. Smudge and Solomon, his thirteen-year-old dogs, followed us. Becky, Geoff, and I looked for the right light and location near the pool while Draper went upstairs to shave his five o'clock shadow.

As Becky and Geoff tried to arrange the dogs in the photograph, Draper's contagious chuckles kept us all laughing. After the session we sat by the pool and discussed his life and his career. When I asked him why he'd gone into government, he replied, "It was a new beginning [with Reagan], and I could afford to, thanks to my previous venture capital business. I have always felt a pull toward Washington because my father was so active in the government, and I felt the need to make a contribution."

Then I asked Becky, a graduate of Smith College and the Stanford Graduate School of Business, for some adjectives to describe her father. She apologized. "It may sound silly for a thirty-one-year-old daughter to say, but I feel the best word I can use to describe him is 'perfect.'" Draper smiled proudly.

E. E. Ferrey

E

d Ferrey's mission has made an impact on high technology throughout the nation, but most dramatically in Silicon Valley. Over the past twenty-five years he has led the American Electronics Association to a membership of 2800 corporate members, 500 associate members, and an annual budget of $15 million. Formerly the Western Electronic Manufacturers Association (WEMA), AEA is the principal voice of the electronics industry in political issues. A trade association, AEA brings venture capital money to high technology, deals with critical legislative issues, and serves as a networking and training ground for electronics executives. Under Ferrey's guidance the association has successfully lobbied for capital gains and stock-option tax reforms and has grown to national prominence.

As a high-school student in Indiana, Ferrey was interested in public speaking, writing, and playing clarinet and saxophone. In addition to traveling all over the Midwest for band and debating competitions, he edited the school yearbook. He also edited the campus newspaper at Indiana University where he majored in journalism and political science.

Ferrey joined the *Fort Wayne News-Sentinel* after graduating with honors in 1942. He then moved on to radio journalism with WHAS in Louisville and began his first electronics public relations assignment with Farnsworth Television and Radio. "My task was to introduce people to the concept of television viewing, a big challenge in the late forties," Ferrey says. He arrived in California in 1952 and worked in public relations for the next seven and a half years with Lenkurt, now a part of General Telephone and Electronics, before joining WEMA.

At AEA's 1985 annual meeting, Vice-President George Bush presented the association's Medal of Achievement to Ferrey for significant contributions to the advancement of electronics. Considered the highest honor given to U.S. electronics executives, the Medal of Achievement has been presented annually since 1960, when David Packard received the first award.

Ferrey is convinced that Silicon Valley will remain the place with the highest concentration of high-technology expertise. "We have always been ahead and we always will be ahead."

ED FERREY

Ed Ferrey's large office welcomed strangers. It is located on the ground floor at the American Electronics Association headquarters in Palo Alto. Across the room from his spacious desk was a conversation area that could have belonged to a therapist. All that was missing was the box of Kleenex.

Ferrey was generous with his time on a Saturday morning. During the hour we spent talking he proved to be a repository of information about Silicon Valley. It has been his life for more than thirty years.

When I went to his Los Altos Hills ranch-style home for a remake, Ferrey was still excited about receiving the AEA's Medal of Achievement, which had been presented the week before by George Bush. Ferrey said, "He wrote me the nicest letter! He even thanked me for letting him and Barbara share the evening with us. I was very touched." Later he told me, "Sure I'm going to help him with his political campaign. But I'm also helping a Democrat in the state legislature who agrees with the AEA's philosophy on business issues. We've got to get the American electronics business back on its feet."

John Freidenrich

John Freidenrich was born in San Francisco, grew up in Palo Alto, crossed El Camino Real from Palo Alto High School to attend Stanford University, and graduated from Stanford Law School in 1963, following his father and grandfather into the legal profession. Freidenrich took a year off before law school to work for California's Senator Claire Engle in Washington.

In 1968 he became a founding partner of Ware & Freidenrich, a Palo Alto law firm founded by the right attorneys at the right time and place to play a vital role in the growth of Silicon Valley. The firm was close at hand to provide corporate and securities advice to high-technology companies as they organized and raised capital and then went public and when they were acquired by larger corporations.

Freidenrich became as active an investor as he was an attorney. In 1976 he established Bay Partners, the first of four venture capital funds he has formed. He divides his time between venture capital and his law practice. Among his investments are GeoMetrics, Shugart Associates, and Margaux Controls. He also serves as a director of several companies.

An active and generous volunteer, Freidenrich is a director of a number of nonprofit organizations, including the New Children's Hospital at Stanford and the Jewish Community Federation. He is a tireless supporter of Stanford University. "I feel it's very important, especially since I was raised here and made money here, to put something back into the community," Freidenrich says. "It's a sense of obligation, and it's rewarding and fulfilling."

JOHN FREIDENRICH

Freidenrich and his wife, Jill, met me in their driveway and helped carry my gear inside, where we had tea in their sunny breakfast room. We chatted about their two children, modern art, photography, and this book. Both were enthusiastic conversationalists, with Freidenrich deferring to his wife's opinions about their art.

After a tour of the house and perfectly groomed garden, we decided to make the portrait in the pool house decorated with the work of the California artist Jay Phillips and the Mexican sculptor Victor Salmones. Freidenrich, a tall man with a full head of hair, laughed as we discussed the aging process and the effect of gravity on the human body. He told me about the book by Robert Ludlum he was currently reading, then responded modestly to my questions about his time-consuming community service activities and the scholarships he has given to Stanford. I was in the company of a man who cares deeply about his community.

Bill H. Quist (signature)

William R. Hambrecht is the founding partner of Hambrecht and Quist, one of the most respected West Coast investment banking and venture capital firms. He is considered a near-legend among the Silicon Valley entrepreneurs who constantly seek his financial support.

Born in 1935 in Oceanside, New York, the son of a successful Mobil Corporation salesman, Hambrecht grew up on Long Island. He attended Princeton, where he played football and majored in history and economics, graduating cum laude. Later he studied at the University of Chicago Graduate School of Business.

Hambrecht started work in 1958 in a securities firm near Cape Canaveral, selling shares of small technology firms. He moved to San Francisco in 1965 to work for Francis I. duPont Company. On a business trip to San Diego he met George Quist, a venture capitalist with the Bank of America. Frustrated with the cautious management style frequently found in big companies, the two decided to form their own business.

Their firm, established in 1968, specializes in high-growth technology companies. It has flourished, its reputation enhanced by the success of the initial public offerings of stock it has handled. Hambrecht and Quist has provided venture capital, underwritten stock issues, and given management help to more than 150 companies, including Convergent Technologies, VLSI, and People Express. Clients range from institutions such as Yale University and American Express to individual investors.

Following Quist's death in 1982, Hambrecht has continued to run the firm along the lines the two partners had envisioned. The firm now has five offices in the United States and one in London.

Hambrecht lives in San Francisco with his wife, Sally; they have five grown children. His hobbies include raising cymbidium orchids and zinfandel grapes. He also has an interest in politics, claiming he has "a natural affinity for the underdog."

WILLIAM R. HAMBRECHT

After walking along a plushly carpeted, office-lined corridor, I reached Hambrecht's conference room where I waited. He was on the phone. Soon the secretary introduced me to a tall, handsome man who looked the part of a 1956 Princeton football guard. I had read that Hambrecht grows orchids, and I visualized this enormous man bending over the delicate blossoms. I commented on how unusual it would have been back in the macho 1950s for a football player to be an orchid grower. Hambrecht agreed. "Men have come a long way. Or at least, our perception of what men ought to do has come a long way."

I must admit it was fun for a small woman to ask this large, strong person to sit here, put his elbow there, turn his head that way. He suggested having his photograph made in front of the sign of one of the new companies he's backed. We did that, then we took some marvelous, relaxed close-ups in front of a plaque that read "Chalone," the name of a vineyard in which Hambrecht has a financial interest. He told me about some of his good wines, and then the subject changed to children. I asked if any of his children attended Princeton. He said, "No, they like California too much to leave." When I asked Hambrecht to sit on the side of his desk, he carefully—even gingerly—moved his family pictures. Picking up several framed snapshots, he told me about some of the people and occasions: a ski trip, a birthday party, a family portrait.

As I walked back down the long hall, I reflected on that simple incident. It seemed that those pictures were not just office decorations. They were silent statements about this man's values.

Pitch Johnson

Franklin Pitcher Johnson, Jr.—almost universally known as Pitch—was born in Quincy, Illinois, in 1928. His father was a track and field coach who competed as a hurdler in the 1924 Olympics in Paris. The family moved to Palo Alto in 1940 when Johnson's father left Drake University to become the Stanford track coach.

Johnson entered Stanford to major in physics, but a summer job in a steel mill introduced him to production and inspired him to change his major to mechanical engineering. At Stanford he was a track and field athlete, specializing in the quarter mile. Johnson earned a B.S.M.E. at Stanford and an M.B.A. at Harvard and served in the air force from 1952 to 1954. He then worked for eight years as an open-hearth production executive for Inland Steel Company.

Recognizing that it was difficult to accumulate capital on a corporate salary and option plans, Johnson decided to move into the higher risk, higher return venture capital arena in 1962. Together he and William Draper formed the successful firm, Draper and Johnson Investment Company. Subsequently, in 1965 Johnson founded Asset Management Company. In the last twenty years, Asset Management has invested in over 100 ventures in a wide variety of technology-based businesses, including Tandem Computers, Applied BioSystems, and Coherent. Johnson currently serves as chairman of the board of the software company Boole and Babbage and is a director of several other companies, including AmGen, Teradyne, and Ross Stores.

An active participant in educational endeavors, Johnson has taught a course in entrepreneurship at Stanford Graduate School of Business since 1979 and works on numerous fundraising and advisory projects for Stanford.

The versatile Johnson enjoys fly fishing, running, opera, and piloting his own plane. His lifelong enthusiasm for track and field events continues. He has traveled all over the world to attend meets, including five Olympic Games.

PITCH JOHNSON

Although it was a rainy day, this former collegiate track man had just completed his thrice-weekly run of several miles and let me make his portrait "as is." We began in his study, near a 1605 Bible which sat next to *The Whole Earth Catalog*. Only in California, I thought. Then we stepped across the room to a family chess table. I wondered aloud if he plays the game with his sons or wife. "No, I don't know a thing about the game." But the light there was soft, and it seemed a relaxing setting for his portrait.

Johnson talked ebulliently about higher education, the Olympics, our sons (who were Palo Alto High School friends), and, eventually, other Silicon Valley pioneers whose names were new to me.

Knowing that his wife, Cathie (who has an M.B.A. and has been actively involved in Asset Management), had researched and published a poster charting the genealogy of West Coast venture capital, I asked to use it in a possible photograph. We went outside to set something up. As we walked around the garden, the Johnsons' sixteen-year-old dog decided he needed some attention and joined us. Although we didn't use that picture, I loved the fact that a venture capitalist had named his dog Midas.

Tom A. Kelley

Tom A. Kelley runs a Silicon Valley executive search firm that recruits management personnel vital to the industrial ferment of high-technology ventures.

Kelley was born in 1939 in Memphis, where he was raised by his mother and grandmother. A talented athlete and good student, he was offered five academic scholarships. He chose Rice University and earned a B.S. in mechanical engineering in 1962. While at Rice he spent a summer working at Yosemite National Park where he met his wife, Sharon. In 1967 he received an M.B.A. from Stanford.

Kelley worked for Trane Company and Raychem Corporation, and then "an inordinate desire to be independent" led him to start Thomas A. Kelley and Associates in 1969. The firm specializes in executive searches for small- to medium-sized high-technology companies. Kelley particularly enjoys getting involved in startup firms and maintaining relationships as those companies grow. Among his long-term clients, perhaps the best known is ROLM, for whom he has conducted executive and professional talent searches for fifteen years.

Kelley thinks some investors in the early 1980s put more emphasis on marketing their high-tech companies than on building them. "This occasionally manifested itself in executive search assignments in which the investor or board member would attach more importance to the image projected by candidates than to the substance of their abilities and experience," he says. "I tell such clients that I know some outstanding businessmen who are really pretty ugly!"

In addition to his recruiting business, Kelley is involved in numerous commercial real-estate holdings throughout the Bay Area. He has also invested in some of his high-tech client companies. In 1985 he was elected a trustee of the Portola Valley School District. Kelley's personal credo is, "I have only wanted to be the best at what I do."

TOM A. KELLEY

His colonial-style home in the foothills offered many possibilities for casual photographs, but I knew I wanted to make Kelley's portrait with his Kennedy memorabilia because he had been a fervent supporter of Jack and Bobby. In addition to Kennedy photographs and sculptures, I think Kelley owns every biography written about the Kennedy family members. And they were all in his study. That was the place for the portrait.

Kelley's laugh is like a little boy's—fresh and infectious. He was easy to talk to and easy to be with. As we were photographing, his eight-year-old daughter, Kathleen, peeked in and asked her dad about an essay on flamingos that she was writing for her third-grade class. He advised her to look in the encyclopedia, then said, "She knows what to do. She just wants to watch." I thought that if I hadn't been there he would have jumped up to guide her and loved every minute of it.

R

egis McKenna is the man who markets Silicon Valley. As chairman and founder of Regis McKenna, Inc., the Valley's most heralded marketing and communications firm, he lectures on, invests in, and champions Silicon Valley.

Born in Pittsburgh, McKenna grew up in a devoutly Roman Catholic family with six brothers, four of whom became priests or monks. He studied literature and existential philosophy at Duquesne University and believes those subjects were of tremendous value to him. "Phenomenology takes an unprejudiced view of reality; existentialism insists that you are what you do. So I gather mountains of information before making judgments, and I urge companies to create their own realities."

While attending Duquesne McKenna worked as a janitor at a girl's high school. There he could enjoy the free food in the kitchen and spend leisure time writing and surrounding himself with 300 young women—one of whom, Dianne Page, a year later became his wife. "It's the best job I ever had," he says.

In 1967 National Semiconductor recruited him as marketing services manager. Charles Sporck, National's president, pays high tribute to McKenna's contribution to the company's early growth.

McKenna started Regis McKenna, Inc. in 1970 with a typewriter and $500. Important accounts include Intel, Genentech, Tandem, Sperry, 3M, and Philips, but perhaps his most famous client is Apple Computer. Approached by Steve Jobs to do advertising and public relations for the fledgling company, McKenna invested both marketing and PR skills in Apple, which soared to the top of the new computer market within three years.

A Democrat, McKenna's political interests included advisory and active support of Gary Hart's presidential candidacy. (His wife, Dianne, is also involved in politics, currently serving as a Santa Clara County Supervisor.) McKenna is an active member of the National Commission on Industrial Innovation (NCII) and the Berkeley Roundtable on Industrial Economy (BRIE). Steve Jobs predicts that McKenna will someday be White House press secretary.

REGIS McKENNA

After waiting forty-five minutes, I was introduced to McKenna, who apologized, saying, "I was on the phone setting up Sunday's campaign breakfast with Gary Hart." (Our photography session occurred several days before the 1984 California primary.) McKenna came into the hallway where I had stationed my camera in front of several framed *Fortune* magazine covers. Although he was obviously in a hurry, he was able to shift gears rapidly and was willing to take directions. (This was not true of everyone I photographed for the book.) I followed McKenna into his large office, whose dark walls featured a lovely Folon silkscreen and a series of color photographs he had taken of his son, daughter, and a neighborhood friend. Two more photographs of an old man and a child standing in a Beirut storefront hung on the wall. This was definitely a people-oriented man. His open leather briefcase sat on the side of his desk, its contents tidily arranged. Nestled in one of the corners, easily accessible, were two packages of M&Ms. I was happy to meet a fellow chocoholic, but he explained they were for emergency use in case of an insulin attack.

We walked outside his office to the staircase of the nautical-looking building, where we made more photographs. When we finished I asked McKenna to look over the list of people I planned to include in the book. He made several enthusiastic suggestions. I listened intently, recognizing that if Regis McKenna wrote a bestseller called *The Regis Touch*, he must know what he's talking about.

Burt McMurtry

B

urton John McMurtry was born in 1935 in Houston, where his father was employed by Humble Oil Company. During his summer vacations McMurtry worked as a laborer in the oil fields. "I enjoyed the physical exertion of the manual work and the satisfaction of seeing something tangible accomplished," he says. But the experience also convinced him that he wanted an education and the opportunity to work with his mind.

In high school Burt McMurtry excelled in academics and the great Texas sport, football. He graduated early and enrolled in Rice Institute (now University) to major in electrical engineering. Entering Rice's five-year program, he earned a B.A. in 1956 and a B.S.E.E. a year later. "The most useful subject was English," McMurtry claims, "because of the importance of communication in virtually every business activity."

While interviewing for jobs at the Rice placement center, McMurtry approached a Sylvania interviewer because "he looked lonesome; no one else was around his booth." This chance conversation led to an offer, and he moved to Mountain View in 1957. He stayed with Sylvania for twelve years, during which time he earned an M.S. and a Ph.D. in electrical engineering at Stanford on the Honors Co-op Program.

In 1969, McMurtry joined Jack Melchor in a seed capital operation and served as president of Palo Alto Investment Company for three years. He then became a partner with Reid Dennis and Burgess Jamieson in Institutional Venture Associates. In 1980 he began his own venture capital firm, Technology Venture Investors with Jim Bochnowski and Dave Marquardt. Over the years he has established a remarkable track record, including investments in ROLM, Triad, and NBI.

"Venture capital is tough, but interesting," McMurtry says. "There are tremendous successes, huge failures." Drawing a parallel between venture capital and his old sport of football, he observes, "Both are event and team oriented. In football, each player has his own role, yet each play depends on the whole team. This is true of the venture capital business as well."

BURTON J. McMURTRY

McMurtry's wife, Deedee, told me we could get the most relaxed photographs of Burt at their Pajaro Dunes beach house, an hour and a half's drive from Silicon Valley.

Reputed to be an intense and driven man, McMurtry showed me another side. As I set up the camera he talked about his new grandchild and his son's acceptance into Stanford's graduate program in mechanical engineering. McMurtry is a guru to many in the Valley because he helps people make critical decisions about their careers, so I asked about that. He explained that he enjoys giving advice to people who seriously want to advance in the electronics industry.

When I inquired about the country's present profusion of venture capitalists, he said, "I think it's good. It gives more people a chance to create and to see their dreams and expectations come to fruition. That can't be bad. It's good for our country and eventually for the progress of the world."

At this point we completed the photographing and all sat in front of the fireplace with the mesmerizing waves repeatedly pounding in the background. We sipped McMurtry's favorite California wine for that year, a magnificent chardonnay, brought to the beach from his impressive Portola Valley wine cellar. The intense venture capitalist seemed completely at ease.

Jack L. Melchor

Early in his life, Jack L. Melchor set goals for himself. He planned to earn $100,000 by the time he was thirty, get married, have four children, and make $1 million before his fortieth birthday. Although he did not reach the first milestone, he did achieve the others.

The sixth of thirteen children, Melchor was the only member of his family to finish high school. Born in 1925 in a tiny North Carolina town, he attended six schools before finishing second grade. When he was seventeen years old he was accepted by the naval officer training program and entered the University of North Carolina. He wanted to broaden himself by taking Spanish and geography, so he carried twenty-six hours of credit. Then he attended midshipmen's school and served in the Pacific. After the war he took advantage of the GI Bill to finish his schooling and received his bachelor's and master's degrees in physics from the University of North Carolina and a Ph.D. in physics from Notre Dame.

In 1953 Melchor joined Sylvania Electric Products in the heart of what would become Silicon Valley. He left Sylvania to start Melabs, a manufacturer of electronic subsystems, and then founded HP Associates (in partnership with Hewlett-Packard). A pioneer in the field of light-emitting diodes, the company was so successful that HP bought him out earlier than expected.

After "retirement" from corporate life in 1968, Melchor formulated a plan that led to a venture capital partnership with Burt McMurtry less than a year later. His many successes include Triad Systems and Verbatim. Melchor's willingness to back unproven entrepreneurs has led him to take chances others will not. Ken Oshman, ROLM's president and cofounder, says, "Who but Jack would have invested in a startup company headed by a twenty-nine-year-old laser researcher?" ROLM, one of the Valley's most spectacular successes, was the result. When asked how he decides which ventures to back, Melchor says he looks at the people involved.

His pastimes are cerebral, not physical. However, in an act that belies his claim of physical inactivity, Melchor recently invited his three-year-old granddaughter to join him in a one-hour dance class on the grounds of Hawaii's Mauna Kea Hotel. "Fortunately," he says, "the rain intervened and we didn't have to go."

JACK L. MELCHOR

Being in Jack Melchor's presence is like being at a Neil Simon play: one minute you're laughing, and the next you're contemplating some universal truth.

I was in Melchor's office several times during the preparation of this book. During the first visit I saw a fun-loving but tense man who conducted his business from an overstuffed chair, his telephone on a small table on one side and his ashtray on a table on the other. Papers, brochures, and prospectuses stacked on the floor in front of his chair told me he had a lot on his mind, and I began to realize he was damned well going to get through the whole pile before he went home that day. It seemed appropriate to photograph him at this "desk."

The next time I visited his office was with the researcher for this book. I had told her she was in for a treat: Melchor recites Chaucer, reads Travis McGee books, enjoys frivolity, and is great with quips. But when we questioned him about his background, there was no comic relief as we heard about his growing up wretchedly poor and migrating to Texas from North Carolina with his family when he was a little boy. Melchor's children, who have heard the stories many times, affectionately and lightheartedly tease him about having lived on corn three times a day. But to us it was new, revealing, and moving.

Thomas Perkins became a venture capitalist after investing $15,000—money that had been earmarked to purchase a home—in University Laboratories, a company he founded. When the venture resulted in a $2 million return he was hooked. Since then he has invested in and helped manage many companies, including Genentech, Tandem, and LSI Logic. "In the 1800s, capitalists invested in steel and railroads," Perkins says. "Those were the high-technology, innovative industries of the day. More recently, it has become science and electronics."

The son of an insurance company adjuster, Perkins was born in Illinois in 1932 and grew up in White Plains, New York. One of his mentors was a high-school physics teacher who encouraged him to apply to MIT and continue his studies in physics. When he encountered "true physics geniuses," however, he changed his major to electrical engineering. He attended Harvard Business School, where professor Georges Doriot was another major influence. Perkins's career has included a variety of successes: corporate management with Hewlett-Packard; teaching at Stanford Graduate School of Business; consulting with Booz, Allen and Hamilton; and his partnership with Kleiner, Perkins, Caufield and Byers.

One of his partners, Frank Caufield, says of Perkins, "Tom thinks big. Psychologically, he is able to push all his chips to the middle of the table." But Perkins explains that instincts and hunches are part of the business. "It's not terribly scientific. I sometimes think that if people knew how we do this, they wouldn't give us all that money."

Perkins owns one of the world's best vintage automobile collections, including Bugattis, Alfa Romeos, and Mercedes Benzes. He drives in rallies in England and Europe and recently published *Supercharged Sports Cars,* a book describing his collection. "I don't turn on to the latest electronic gadget," he explains. "I turn on to older, nonelectrical things."

A strong believer in employee ownership of companies, Perkins says, "In just about every company I'm involved with, every employee is a shareholder."

THOMAS PERKINS

Tom Perkins strolled into his office at 10 o'clock sharp. He's one of the few people in the book I saw "stroll." Someone inquired about last night's ballet and he replied, "Great!" After our introduction, he asked me if he had time to get a soft drink. Back he strolled with a can in his hand, opened it, and sat down where I pointed. I was delighted to make a portrait of this powerful venture capitalist holding a humble can of tomato juice.

From our vantage point in a glass room inside Perkins's glass and chrome Palo Alto office I could see other people watching and waiting. So we had a brief session. Nevertheless, we chatted about his then-recent photograph in *TIME*, his antique automobile collection, classical music radio stations, and his favorite book of the moment, *Autumn of the Patriarch.* (I wanted to ask him what his wife, Gerd, had thought about his using the down payment for their house as an investment in something else, but I didn't have the courage.) That we could cover so many subjects in so few minutes amazed me, but Perkins thinks and answers rapidly. As I packed up he said, "Is that all? That was quick and painless." By now he had changed into his business self. He didn't stroll out. Into the rhythm of a typical day, he bounded out to welcome his first business visitor.

O ne of Sanford R. Robertson's most deeply ingrained memories is his father's oft-repeated advice, "You're never going to be happy until you have your own business." In 1978, when Robertson set up his investment banking partnership, the first thing he did was call his seventy-nine-year-old father with the news.

An only child, Robertson was born in 1931 in Chicago, where his father ran a large suburban restaurant. He received a degree in business administration in 1953 and an M.B.A. in 1954 from the University of Michigan, and then he served as a supply officer in the navy. In 1958 he joined American Hospital Supply Corporation. Of that experience he says, "I was bored by being in one company all the time." A year later he joined investment bankers Smith, Barney & Company in New York, rising to vice-president and director. Robertson moved to their San Francisco office in 1965. Four years later he became a founding partner in Robertson, Colman, Siebel & Weisel, now Montgomery Securities. Several of the principals spun off in 1978 to form the present partnership of Robertson, Colman and Stephens.

Sandy Robertson thinks that by starting his own firms he gained important insight for working with entrepreneurs. Two prominent companies that he has brought public are ROLM and Tandem. Anything but bored now, Robertson says, "With each phone call I'm dealing with a different company. I'm changing industry groups all day long."

Of Silicon Valley's future he says, "Silicon Valley has the critical mass to continue being the most important technology center in the world. We may not grow larger from a manufacturing standpoint, but the talent that's here will keep it strong and vital."

SANDY ROBERTSON

I had to wait a long time in Sandy Robertson's office, but he dashed in every ten minutes to apologize for his unexpected meeting. In the meantime I was able to walk around and see his firm's great collection of modern art: Jim Dine, Franz Kline, and several other famous painters. On the wall nearest his desk I noticed photographs of three lovely looking women with enough resemblance to Robertson that I knew they were his daughters.

As we photographed, he told me about people he considered outstanding in Silicon Valley, loaning me his Mont Blanc pen to make notes. When I asked him to stand by the Joan Miro abstract sculpture of a bull, he related to me that he bought and enjoyed it for its "bullish symbolism."

I felt that the photographs we took that day were too officelike, so we tried a few months later at his home in Sausalito. The hillside house stood on stilts, looking directly over the sailboats and toward San Francisco Bay. This time, Robertson had just returned from a run with his wife Jeanne—up and down several miles of hills—and they both looked invigorated.

Robertson was generous with his time and let me photograph him near his telescope, on the sundeck, in the wine cellar, and in front of the Japanese screen he had recently commissioned by one of Japan's "national treasures," Shiryu Morita. He was relaxed, and it was nice to have Jeanne there to cheer him on.

Arthur Rock

Arthur Rock is acknowledged by his peers as "the top player in the game." At the same time, he shuns publicity and is intensely discreet. Since the late 1950s, when he and partner Tommy Davis formed one of the first venture capital firms to invest in Silicon Valley, Rock has been a leader in this particularly American branch of finance.

The son of a candy-store owner in Rochester, New York, Rock was born in 1926. After graduating from Syracuse University with a degree in business and attending Harvard Business School, he began his career on Wall Street. He now lives and works in San Francisco and Aspen, Colorado.

Rock is a disciplined and analytical businessman, averaging only three to four investments a year. Not considered a gambler, he is cautious in his approach. He becomes totally involved with a company once he's made the commitment. Among the more spectacularly successful of these commitments have been Fairchild Semiconductor, Intel, and Apple Computer.

Admittedly old-fashioned, he has no use for television. He has been a Giants baseball fan for twenty-five years and also attends the opera and ballet, supports the San Francisco Museum of Modern Art, and is a collector of contemporary art. A bout of polio contracted as a child does not prevent him from enjoying skiing.

Rock is seen by some as gentle and charming; others find him awesome. Andrew Grove says, "Art Rock is like the pilot of a plane who sees the geography far better than the people who are driving around in it."

ARTHUR ROCK

No name appears on Rock's San Francisco office door, just his office number. A single old-fashioned radiator in the reception room contrasts with the Mark Adams tapestry. In spite of the aura of "Arthur Rock, a *TIME* cover-story man" for an issue featuring the venture capital business, I felt completely at ease in his office. His soft-spoken secretary of twenty years, Marie Getchel, greeted me like I was a regular visitor.

Rock rushed in from lunch a little early, shifted gears quickly, and was immediately ready for our appointment. I needed a few more minutes to set up lights, so I told him he had time to make a phone call. When I was ready, he cooperated fully. He even sat gently on the radiator for one picture. Although I was not after smiling photographs, I got one when I said, "We'll make a picture for your wife."

Rock was congenial and straightforward. We discussed his art collection, especially the pre-Columbian figures. But I didn't dilly-dally. I finished and left before my promised time of half an hour had elapsed. He went back to his desk. As I was packing up my gear, I looked at that door I've read about—the unmarked door. So I asked Marie if Mr. Rock might dash out for one more picture, standing in the doorway. He did, and we got a photograph we both like. Maybe his wife likes it, too.

Larry W. Sonsini

Lawrence W. Sonsini once considered a career in medicine, but by his junior year at the University of California at Berkeley, he realized he wanted more flexibility than he felt medicine would allow. He found that he enjoyed economics and government courses, so he entered the university's Boalt Hall School of Law in 1963.

Born in 1941, Sonsini spent his early years in Rome, New York, until his father's job with Hughes Aircraft caused the family to move to Los Angeles in 1949. At Cal he played football and rugby through his sophomore year, recruited athletes, and announced freshman basketball and football games.

Sonsini was greatly influenced by Richard W. Jennings, a Boalt professor in securities law—a specialty Jennings believed was not being heavily practiced in Silicon Valley. Sonsini came to the Peninsula, where he met John Wilson, Pete McCloskey, and Roger Mosher, who were then practicing together. The firm's informal atmosphere and emphasis on representing new businesses appealed to Sonsini, and the partners were impressed with his corporate securities knowledge. He joined them in 1966. Principally by providing legal services to growing Silicon Valley companies in corporate law, securities, and mergers and acquisitions, the firm (now known as Wilson, Sonsini, Goodrich and Rosati) has grown to approximately ninety lawyers.

A key adviser to many successful Silicon Valley companies, Sonsini serves on the boards of directors of several. Recently he began teaching part time at Boalt, where he has taken over Professor Jennings's classes in securities law.

Sonsini admires the entrepreneurial spirit in Silicon Valley that has allowed people of varying backgrounds to be involved at all levels. "I believe that the Valley will remain influential in the fostering of new businesses," he says, "but that which is already here will continue to bring forth new challenges."

LARRY W. SONSINI

When I walk into an office I usually get a feeling for how much time I'll probably have. Here, I knew I had to work fast.

Larry Sonsini was polite but hurried when he arrived for our appointment. No idle talk. No banter. I had hoped to photograph him on the golf course, but instead we worked in his office. His desk was perfectly organized, with files set at exact angles to each other, in order of the day's priorities, I assumed. The business-like photographing session was one of my shortest for this book—eight minutes.

The next time I met Sonsini, in a purely social setting, I had the opportunity to observe a more informal side of the man. He was affable, witty, charming, and a marvelous listener as he elicited information from an eager young mother about her children. I understood why he has such devoted clients as well as good friends.

John A. Wilson

John Arnot Wilson is the founder of Wilson, Sonsini, Goodrich and Rosati, the largest law firm with headquarters in Silicon Valley.

Born in Akron, Ohio, where his father was an executive in the rubber industry, Wilson attended boarding school at Western Reserve Academy. At Princeton he majored in history and attended the School of Public and International Affairs. When he began to plan his future, he concluded that he would rather be a professional than a businessman. "Law was the right course for me," he says. He received a law degree from Yale just as World War II was beginning, and then he enlisted in the navy and served for four years as a pilot and instructor.

He came to love California while stationed at Moffett Field, in the heart of the Santa Clara Valley. But after the service, Wilson returned to Ohio to practice law in Cleveland. He later accepted a post with the Atomic Energy Commission, finding Washington, D.C., fascinating but out of touch with the "grass roots." He left government and came to Palo Alto to join Hiller Aircraft Corporation. After three years he abandoned the corporate scene to establish his own law practice. He continued to serve as legal counsel to Hiller, which became his first client.

Wilson particularly enjoys working with businessmen and has participated in the incorporation or early organization of a large number of the Valley's high-technology companies, including Coherent, ESL, and ROLM.

He believes the Valley is becoming a principal focal point of the country because of its business, financial, educational, and cultural attractions. "This is a mixed blessing," he says. "From the viewpoint of material progress, it's good, but we need to be careful to organize and contain the growth."

JOHN A. WILSON

Commanding the top floor of one of the area's tallest buildings, John Wilson's law firm overlooks Stanford University and its rolling hills—a spectacular Peninsula view.

Wilson came into his spacious, newly decorated lobby right on time, introduced himself, and helped carry my equipment back to his office. He was tall, with kindly eyes that looked intently at me as I spoke. His conversation was so friendly and open that I hardly remember making the portrait.

We talked about the Indian necklace I was wearing, art, his children, and his early days as a lawyer. His nonslick look and naturalness fascinated me. Nevertheless, I didn't ask him about the leather belt he had on that looked like he'd worn since law school. The belt was a wonderfully human contrast to the reputation and setting of this dignified man and his distinguished law firm.

Jack W Yelverton

As owner and president of Yelverton and Company in San Francisco, Jack Yelverton has recruited more presidents for Silicon Valley firms than has any other executive search consultant.

The son of a locomotive engineer, Yelverton was born in Douglas, Arizona, in 1930. After receiving a B.S. in industrial management from Arizona State University and an M.B.A. from New York University, he joined Bechtel Corporation in San Francisco as an industrial engineer. In 1958 he moved to Fairchild Semiconductor, where he became director of personnel and later division director of administration.

At Fairchild Yelverton worked with Bob Noyce to establish ground rules for employee relations in the fast-paced, rapidly changing setting of a high-technology company. He hoped to develop a structure in which employer and employee could cooperate in an intense environment characterized by frequent changes in priorities, products, and personnel. "We wanted less structure and less confrontation than there is in the traditional East Coast business world," he says. The kind of egalitarian system with open communication that he and Noyce developed became a model for later companies and is now widely accepted as one of the hallmarks of Silicon Valley businesses.

In 1961 Yelverton joined five colleagues to form Signetics Corporation, an integrated circuit manufacturing company. Four years later he left manufacturing to help develop Wilkinson, Sedwick and Yelverton, Inc., one of the six largest search firms in the United States. Later he became the firm's president. In the late 1970s Yelverton reduced the company to the single office that he now operates as Yelverton and Company.

Yelverton balances his serious business side with a playful sense of humor. He attacks his leisure activities with the same ferocity with which he pursues his work. He is a long-distance runner, swimmer, and tennis player as well as a hunter and fisherman. As an ocean sailor, he once tied himself to the tiller to bring his boat home single-handedly through a gale. In quieter moments he has planted his own vineyard. Don Dedera, a friend of Yelverton and editor of *Arizona Highways,* says, "Jack does not know everything. He simply knows everything he needs to know."

JACK YELVERTON

Some office! It looks right into San Francisco's Transamerica pyramid and is at nearly the same height. Jack Yelverton looked a part of this setting with his three-piece pinstripe suit and watch chain, and with the air of confident contentment that I saw in many of these successful men.

A pleasant man who listens to the PBS Morning Edition on his way to work and who in his spare time was reading Barbara Tuchman's *A Distant Mirror,* Yelverton patiently waited while I set up cameras and lights and did test shots in front of his windows. After I photo-graphed him in his conference room, we walked ten steps to his next-door office with another magnificent view of San Francisco. This room was more personal. A model sailboat gave the clue to Yelverton's hobby, but I could hardly picture him as the sailor in his friend's raging-sea story—tying himself to the tiller. Then he looked up from his desk. There was a faint glint of mischief, adventure, and daring. Now I could visualize Jack Yelverton fighting the elements all alone on the ocean. The business world itself is not exactly a sea of tranquility.

Ed Zschau is called the Silicon Valley congressman. Not only does his district include a large portion of the Valley, but he also founded a successful high-technology company himself before he entered Congress.

As chairman of the American Electronics Association, Zschau led the successful fight to reduce the capital gains tax in 1978. While campaigning to reduce that tax he taped and distributed to members of Congress a song he wrote entitled "The Old Risk Capital Blues." Zschau's efforts helped to achieve a 50 percent reduction in the tax, triggering a new and sustained boom in venture capital for starting new enterprises.

First elected to the U.S. House of Representatives in 1982, Zschau found that Washington politicians wanted to encourage high technology but knew little about exactly how to do it. As chairman of the new House Republican Task Force on High Technology Initiatives, he helped steer government policy toward creating an environment in which innovation and entrepreneurship can flourish.

During his first term Zschau was named "Rookie of the Year" by *Washington Monthly*. The respected *Congressional Quarterly* called him "high tech's premier ambassador to Washington."

Zschau graduated cum laude from Princeton in 1961 with an A.B. in philosophy, and he earned M.B.A., M.S., and Ph.D. degrees at Stanford. Zschau was a professor for five years at the Stanford Graduate School of Business and for one year was a visiting professor at the Harvard Business School. In 1968 he founded System Industries, a disk-memory manufacturer.

Born in Omaha in 1940, Zschau maintains his folksy, Midwestern style. He is the Bay Area's only Republican congressman and works with the administration and members of Congress from both parties to enact his carefully crafted legislative agenda.

Zschau served two terms in the House and is running for the Senate in 1986. In explaining that decision, he reiterates his belief in the Jeffersonian model of public service—that an effective Congress requires regular injections of fresh members.

ED ZSCHAU

Schedules are made and followed exactly in this office. Efficiency was in the air along with a calm, relaxed attitude not found in all Silicon Valley offices.

Zschau is an average-sized man with a whimsical smile that plays at the corners of his mouth. I had a vague feeling that he was about to burst forth with a clever ditty, but I suppose that would have been inappropriate for a congressman, even when he's being photographed casually.

The House vote on the MX missile was approaching, and Ed Zschau was doing his homework. He had been attending meetings and listening nonstop to his constituents on both sides of the question. He seemed to absorb information easily. On one occasion, someone had suggested he read a particular book to learn more about the Russian people. I understand that he bought the book the next day and read it on his return flight to Washington.

I photographed Zschau at his Sunnyvale office one Saturday morning. He looked slightly rumpled, like he had already put in a long day. But I liked that lack of spit-and-polish appearance. He seemed real.

GLOSSARY

ABACUS An ancient device comprised of a frame and beads used for counting; originated in China and used in other Asian countries.

AEA American Electronics Association; a trade organization for the electronics industry; its headquarters and largest concentration of members are in Silicon Valley.

AI Artificial intelligence; a part of computer science; the objective is to build machines that can plan, reason, and perceive.

ARPA Advanced Research Projects Agency (now DARPA, for Defense); the sponsor of much pioneering research and development.

AUDION A vacuum tube having three electrodes; invented by Lee DeForest in Palo Alto in 1906.

BINARY NUMBERS A numbering system based on two numbers, 1 and 0 (in contrast with the base-ten decimal system that is used in day-to-day counting).

BIT A single binary number, either 0 or 1.

BYTE A cluster of bits (usually eight).

CEO Chief executive officer of a company.

CHIP A semiconductor device, usually an integrated circuit. The word *chip* comes from the appearance of the small die, which contains a collection of very large numbers of extremely small interconnected circuit elements such as transistors, diodes, resistors, and capacitors. Most chips are silicon, but some devices use gallium arsenide or germanium.

CIRCUIT BOARD A board, typically fiberglass, with interconnecting electrical conductors, on which electronic devices such as integrated circuits, resistors, and capacitors are mounted; these are building blocks of electronic equipment such as computers and television sets.

COO Chief operating officer.

DAISY-WHEEL PRINTER A typewriterlike printing device with characters arranged on a wheel in a daisylike pattern.

DEGREES AND MAJORS:

A.B., B.A.	Bachelor of arts.
B.B.A.	Bachelor of business administration.
B.S.	Bachelor of science.
Ch.E.	Chemical engineering.
C.S.	Computer science.
E.E.	Electrical engineering.
M.A.	Master of arts.
M.B.A.	Master of business administration.
M.E.	Mechanical engineering.
M.S.	Master of science.
M.S.E.E.	Master of science in electrical engineering.
Ph.D.	Doctor of philosophy (used as the title for an advanced degree in the arts and humanities as well as in science and engineering).

DIGITAL COMPUTER A symbol-processing device that makes use of digits, usually 0 and 1; almost all electronic computers are digital rather than analog.

DIODE An electronic device that passes current in only one direction; a commonly used circuit element.

DISK DRIVE A storage device that uses a magnetically coated rotating disc to store computer data; because the stored information is so rapidly accessible compared with magnetic tape data, this development was critical to the growth of computer usage.

ELECTRICITY The phenomenon associated with the movement of subatomic charged particles.

ELECTRONICS The study and design of equipment based on the control of electric currents by manipulation of electric charges, especially electrons.

EXPERT SYSTEMS Computer systems that learn and mimic the decision-making processes of human experts in various fields.

GERMANIUM A chemical element often used to make certain kinds of semiconductor devices; the first transistors were made with germanium.

IC Integrated circuit.

IEEE Institute of Electrical and Electronics Engineers; an international technical professional society.

INTEGRATED CIRCUIT Electronic device in which all the circuit elements (such as transistors, diodes, resistors, and capacitors) are contained and interconnected on a single semiconductor die (chip) instead of having separate components wired together. ICs are much faster, more reliable, and cheaper to build than circuits made with discrete components, and consequently have dominated electronics since they became generally available fifteen years ago; invented independently by Robert Noyce and Jack Kilby.

KLYSTRON TUBE A type of vacuum tube used to generate or amplify microwave signals.

LASER Acronym for light amplification by stimulated emission of radiation; lasers are sources of highly directional monochromatic light and are used in medicine, measurements, materials processing, and defense.

MAINFRAME A large computer, typically serving many users.

MASER Acronym for microwave amplification by stimulated emission of radiation; masers are used as low-noise amplifiers in microwave receivers.

MEMORY CHIP An integrated circuit consisting of semiconductor devices that store information in binary form; the availability of these low-cost, compact devices with their rapidly accessible data storage was critical to the enormous growth of the use of computers.

MICROPROCESSOR An integrated circuit that provides, in one chip, functions equivalent to those contained in the central processing unit of a computer. A microprocessor interprets and executes instructions and usually incorporates arithmetic capabilities and some memory.

MICROWAVES Electromagnetic radiation in the frequency range from approximately 1 to 30 gigahertz (1GHz is one billion cycles per second); ordinary FM broadcast radio waves are in the 0.1GHz range.

MICROWAVE TUBE A vacuum-tube device that amplifies or generates microwave radiation.

MOORE'S LAW The accurate and durable prediction made by Gordon Moore in the early 1960s that the complexity of integrated circuits would double annually; he modified it in the late 1970s to predict a doubling every two years; when Moore announced his law, there were but a few transistors per chip; by 1985 manufacturers were introducing chips with more than a million transistors each and Moore's Law is still reliable.

MOUSE A device for entering certain computer commands; rolling the mouselike device on a desk causes analogous movement of the cursor on a computer video display, and buttons on the mouse can be used to deliver commands to the computer when the cursor is at the proper location, thus reducing the use of a keyboard.

NATIONAL ACADEMY OF ENGINEERING Highly selective national honorary society recognizing contributions in engineering.

NATIONAL ACADEMY OF SCIENCES Highly selective national society recognizing contributions in the physical and natural sciences.

NOBEL PRIZE The highly prestigious award given annually to individuals for outstanding work in a variety of fields; awarded to encourage work for the interests of humanity.

OSCILLATORS Electronic devices that produce electrical signals at selected, sometimes adjustable, frequencies.

PERIPHERALS Pieces of equipment such as printers and memory-storage devices that assist computers in doing their job.

PERSONAL COMPUTER (PC) An inexpensive computer designed to be owned and used by an individual.

PLANAR PROCESS A way of interconnecting several tiny transistors and other components on silicon during the manufacturing process of the chips; was a commercial breakthrough because the transistors and other circuit elements did not have to be cut apart physically and wired back together again; invented by Jean Hoerni.

RADAR Acronym for radio detection and ranging; system that uses the echoes of electromagnetic waves bounced off targets (such as airplanes, missiles, and automobiles) to determine their location and/or velocity.

RADIATION CHEMISTRY Use of ionizing radiation to cause changes in the properties of materials.

RANDOM ACCESS Computer memory organized in such a way that any part of it can be retrieved almost instantly (much faster than from a magnetic tape, for example, which must be read sequentially rather than randomly).

SEMICONDUCTOR A material that resists the flow of electric current more than does a conductor but less than does an insulator. Commercial semiconductor devices are usually made of silicon, germanium, or gallium arsenide; such devices are the basis for almost all modern electronics, although cathode-ray tubes (CRTs) continue to be the dominant type of display, and certain microwave functions are presently performed well only by vacuum tubes.

SILICON The semiconductor that is the basic ingredient in the majority of semiconductor electronic devices such as transistors and integrated circuits.

SPECTROSCOPY The study of spectra (that is, the emission, transmission, or absorption as a function of wavelength) chiefly to determine the properties of materials or objects.

SUPERCHIP A very large IC.

TRANSISTOR A semiconductor device that can be used as an amplifier, a switch, or an oscillator; it has replaced the vacuum-tube triode in most applications; invented by John Bardeen, Walter Brattain, and William Shockley in 1947.

TRIODE A three-electrode vacuum tube that can be used as an amplifier, a switch, or an oscillator.

VACUUM TUBE Electronic devices that preceded transistor technology and consist of metallic structures housed in glass, metal, or ceramic tubes from which air has been pumped out; ENIAC and all the early computers used vacuum tubes.

VENTURE CAPITAL Often called risk capital; investment funds used primarily to finance startups or early-stage companies.

WAFER A thin disk of semiconductor material on which many die, or chips, are fabricated at one time; the chips are subsequently separated and packaged individually.

WAFER-SCALE ICs that occupy an entire wafer rather than an individual chip cut from such a wafer.

WEMA Western Electronics Manufacturers Association, the trade association whose name has been changed to American Electronics Association (AEA).

WINDOWING A way of dividing the screen of a computer video display into sections called windows; in some cases the windows can be made to overlap.

WORD PROCESSOR A program that permits a computer to be used as an extremely versatile typewriter that allows text corrections, insertions, rearrangement, and formatting.

BIBLIOGRAPHY

Atanasoff, John Vincent. "Advent of Electronic Digital Computing." *Annals of the History of Computing* (July 1984): 229–82.

Bardeen, John. "Beginnings of Solid State Physics and Engineering." *Bent* (Spring 1985): 34–37.

——— . "To a Solid State." *Science 84* (November 1984): 143–45.

Boraiko, Allen A. "The Chip." *National Geographic* (October 1982): 420–57.

Braun, Ernest, and Stuart MacDonald. *Revolution in Miniature.* Cambridge: Cambridge University Press, 1980.

Cameron, Emmet G. "The Peninsula Electronics Story, Part 1." *IEEE Grid* (December 1984): 5, 10.

——— . "The Peninsula Electronics Story, Part 2." *IEEE Grid* (January 1985): 5.

——— . "The Peninsula Electronics Story, Part 3." *IEEE Grid* (February 1985): 7, 9.

Hoefler, Don C. "Silicon Valley-USA, Part 1." *Electronic News* (11 January 1971): 1, 4–5.

——— . "Silicon Valley-USA, Part 2." *Electronic News* (18 January 1971): 1, 4–5.

——— . "Silicon Valley-USA, Part 3." *Electronic News* (25 January 1971): 1, 3–5.

Freiberger, Paul, and Michael Swaine. *Fire in the Valley.* Berkeley, California: Osborne/McGraw-Hill, 1984.

Galbraith, John Kenneth. *The Anatomy of Power.* Boston: Houghton Mifflin, 1983.

Grove, Andrew. *High Output Management.* New York: Random House, 1983.

Hanson, Dirk. *New Alchemists: Silicon Valley and the Microelectronics Revolution.* Boston: Little, Brown Co., 1982.

Johnston, Moira. "High Tech, High Risk, and High Life in Silicon Valley." *National Geographic* (October 1982): 458–77.

Kidder, Tracy. *Soul of a New Machine.* New York: Avon Books, 1981.

Levering, Robert; Michael Katz; and Milton Moskowitz. *Computer Entrepreneurs: Who's Making It Big and How in America's Upstart Industry.* New York: New American Library, 1984.

Levy, Steven. *Hackers: Heroes of the Computer Revolution.* Garden City, New York: Anchor Press/Doubleday, 1984.

Lustig, Lawrence K., ed. *Impact, A Compilation of Bell System Innovations in Science and Engineering,* 2nd ed. New York: Bell Laboratories, 1981.

Maclean, Norman. *A River Runs Through It and Other Stories.* Chicago: University of Chicago Press, 1976.

Morgan, Jane. *Electronics in the West: The First Fifty Years.* Palo Alto, California: National Press Books, 1967.

Moritz, Michael. *Little Kingdom: The Private Story of Apple Computer.* New York: William Morrow, 1984.

Noyce, Robert. "Microelectronics, *Microelectronics: A Scientific American Book.* San Francisco: W. H. Freeman, 1977: 2–9.

Noyce, Robert N. and Marcian E. Hoff. "History of Microprocessors." *Micro* (February 1981): 8–11, 13–21.

Osborne, Adam, and John Dvorak. *Hypergrowth: The Rise and Fall of Osborne Computer Corporation.* Berkeley, California. Idthekkethan, 1984.

Peters, Thomas J., and Robert H. Waterman, Jr. *In Search of Excellence.* New York: Warner Books, 1982.

Reich, Herbert J. "Electron Tube," *McGraw-Hill Encyclopedia of Electronics and Computers.* New York: McGraw-Hill, 1984: 299.

Reid, T. R. *The Chip.* New York: Simon and Schuster, 1984.

Rogers, E.M., and J. K. Larsen. *Silicon Valley Fever.* New York: Basic Books, 1984.

Shurkin, Joel. *Engines of the Mind.* New York: W. W. Norton, 1984.

Stewart, Jon. "The Rise and Fall of Nolan Bushnell." *California Living* (10 March 1985): 11–15.

Thomas, Shirley. *Men of Space,* Volume 4. Chapter on William Shockley. Radnor, Pennsylvania: Chilton Book Co., 1962.

Turkel, Studs. *Working.* New York: Avon Books, 1975.

U.S. Navy: Bureau of Naval Personnel. *Introduction to Electronics.* New York: Dover Publications, 1965.

Varian, Dorothy. *The Inventor and the Pilot.* Palo Alto, California: Pacific Books, 1983.

Wilson, John W. *The New Venturers.* Reading, Massachusetts: Addison Wesley, 1985.

Wolfe, Tom. "The Tinkerings of Bob Noyce." *Esquire* (December 1983): 346–74.

ACKNOWLEDGMENTS

A first book requires a lot of help. This project is complete thanks to these people: *Don Caddes* for technical information; for moral support and part of the book's financial support for four years; for reading every word before it left our house. *Barbara Newton* for doing most of the biographical research, for having a consistently good sense of humor, and for saying, "Let's get this book going!" *Barbara Oshman* for telling me in 1982, "It's a good idea—do it!" and in 1985, "Finish it!"

I am grateful to those who made a number of pivotal contributions: *Paul Hwoschinsky* for getting me an appointment with Bob Noyce, thus making the book begin to happen. *Jack Melchor* for giving me some key addresses and phone numbers. *Ken Oshman* and *Burton McMurtry* for answering questions each time I asked. *Elliott Sopkin* for arranging my appointment with Jerry Sanders and for his needed cooperation, encouragement, and wit.

Many people helped immeasurably—and at critical times: The late *Ansel Adams* and his workshops for ten years of inspiration and critiques. *Frances Baer* for spotting photographs. *John Bardeen* for his generosity in writing the foreword. The California production team headed by *Mary Borchers* and *Joan Davis,* and which included *Valerie Brewster* on typesetting and *Beverly Kennon-Kelley* on page make-up. *Alain Brie* for assisting with the 1985 portrait of the Fairchild Eight. *Linda Elkind* for arranging lunch with the prospective publisher. *Ed Ferrey* for his time teaching me Silicon Valley's history. *Jim Gibbons* for telling me about the Fairchild Eight and checking the historical data. *Milton Glaser* for accepting the book design job—even before I gave him some California apricots—and to *Susan Huggins* for carrying out the design. *Andrea Hendrick* for her artistic sensibility. *Christy Holloway* and *Susie Crocker* for creative marketing. *Ilford Inc.* for giving me a discount on photographic paper (through *Terry Shuchat* and *Bob Burns*). *Dick Johnson* for telling me vital information about events and people. *Bill Kaufmann* for encouraging creative literary projects in Silicon Valley. *Pat Kollings* for providing book-producing wisdom. *Minnette Lehmann* for photograph consultation. *Alice* and *Greg Melchor* for their confidence and for convincing me that Tom Wolfe would jump at the chance to write the biographies. (Sorry! He was too busy.) *John Newton* for looking up names in *Who's Who. Karen* and *Nils Nilsson* for publishing the book and being—I suspect—the kindest, most rational people in the business. *Carolyn Tajnai* for checking Dr. Terman's biography. *George Williams* for making me promise when I left his creative writing class in 1958 to write a book someday.

Other people provided ongoing encouragement, reassurance, and prodding: *Mary Lee* and *Sid Burrus, Andy Grove, Judith Kays, Sandy Kurtzig, Deedee McMurtry, Art Rock, Jud Scholtz, Ann Swanson, Annita Schwartz* and my two children, *Scott* and *Jill.*

I thank the following people who helped make the text better: *Joan Chace* for refining the manuscript. *Fran Coleberd* for her unselfishness in editing and sharing publishing information. *Jo Combs* for editing the biographies and for her delightful, spicy remarks—expurgated. *Ann Dauer* for sharing her love for words and editing (E. B. White would have appreciated her). *Mary Hughes* for her perception in critiquing the manuscript, and telling me, "Get rid of the slurpiness." *Laura Kenney* for careful copyediting. *Mary Lorey* for listening to what I thought was the final manuscript and asking the right questions before it was too late. *Charlotte MacDonald* for crawling into my mind to check my personal observations.

Without advice from the following people, I would still be seeking the creators of Silicon Valley: *Jim Adams, Ted Costello, Steve Harris, Les Hogan, Tom Kelley, Eugene Kleiner, John Linvill, Jim Meindl, Jim Newton, George* and *Joan Parker, Bill Perry, Cal Quate, Hank* and *Gayle Riggs, Sandy Robertson, Tony Siegman, Jimmy Treybig, Greg Young,* and *Rosemary Young.*

I am indebted to the pioneers for their cooperation throughout this project, including permission to use their signatures.

And I shall always appreciate the polite and patient secretaries who answered my many letters and returned all my phone calls. They, like the wives, are special heroines of Silicon Valley. ■

INDEX

C O L O P H O N

PHOTOGRAPHY

CAMERA	Hasselblad
LENSES	50, 80, and 150 mm
FILM	TriX (rated 320) developed in HC110B
PAPER	Ilford Gallerie developed in Dektol

PUBLICATION

DESIGN	Milton Glaser, Inc., New York
TYPE	Gill Sans, Bodoni, and Bauer Bodoni
PAPER	157 gsm U-lite
TYPOGRAPHY AND PRODUCTION	William Kaufmann, Inc., Los Altos, California
MANUFACTURING COORDINATION	Interprint, San Francisco
PRINTING AND BINDING	Dai Nippon, Tokyo